Experiments and innovations in education No. 4

Understanding change in education: an introduction

A.M. Huberman

School of Psychology and Education
University of Geneva

Unesco : IBE

Published in 1973 by the
United Nations Educational, Scientific
and Cultural Organization
7, place de Fontenoy, 75700 Paris, France

LC. No. 73-78939

English edition ISBN 92-3-101116-2

French edition ISBN 92-3-201116-6
Spanish edition ISBN 92-3-301116-x

Printed by Rolland, Paris
Printed in France

Preface

This study attempts to sum up our present knowledge of the process of innovation in education. It is, in part, a synthesis; and the author points out that he has depended heavily on the American sources which make up the bulk of the writings explicitly concerned with innovation. He approaches this material from an international and comparative point of view and shows the need for more systematic reporting of cases of change from other parts of the world.

But the study is more than a literature survey. In order to provide a guide to the subject, Mr. Huberman examines at some length the concept of innovation. The changes that occur in education may be small or large; in a given system, the change may be the adoption of some practice already used elsewhere - so that an innovation is not necessarily an invention. But what distinguishes an innovation from change in general is the element of deliberate planning or intention. Finally, whether the innovation relates to educational objectives or to some part of the educational process, it must ultimately be understood in terms of human behaviour and relationships.

From this definition, the author goes on to examine the factors and agents at work - both those making for change and those inhibiting it. The greater part of the study is concerned with the mechanism of innovation. This analysis leads finally to the setting out of three models which can, each of them, be used to account for the way certain innovations take place: research and development; social interaction; and problem-solving. In practice, many examples can be found to combine aspects of the three models; but this does not reduce the value of the models as instruments for analysing the innovation process.

The concluding part of the study contains some penetrating remarks on the problem of evaluation. All theories of planned change contain the requirement that the process itself should be continuously evaluated, so that the results may be demonstrated, measured against the initial objectives. Then, when improvement can be shown, it is theoretically likely that the innovation will be adopted, which is to say, repeated on a wider scale. Mr. Huberman points out that in education the innovative project brings about change in the objectives themselves, and this fact must be borne in mind when we are planning for change.

The study, then, is a contribution to our understanding of educational change. No doubt it raises more questions than it answers. This is intentional. But as it stands, the text may well serve as the basis for a valuable seminar in institutions of training and research; or provide a more rapid but stimulating reading for the administrator who wishes to see more clearly how he may strive for qualitative improvements and increased effectiveness in his educational system.

As such, the study forms an important element in the new series of reports which the International Bureau of Education is now launching.

The author, Mr. A.M. Huberman, is a professor in the Geneva University School of Psychology and Educational Sciences and was for some years a member of the Unesco Secretariat. The Secretariat wishes to record its gratitude to him for the time and effort he has devoted to preparing a work of this magnitude.

Table of Contents

Introduction *p. 1*

I.   Definitions: types, sources and processes of innovation *p.1*

  1. A working definition of innovation *p. 5*
  2. General sources of change and enabling factors *p. 7*
  3. Types and degrees of change *p. 9*
  4. Engineering educational change *p. 13*
  5. Introduction to process models *p. 14*

II.   Individuals, groups, institutions, cultures: an overview of the agents involved in change *p. 10*

III. System and process: the major variables *p. 25*

  1. Why schools change so slowly *p. 25*
  2. Curves and rates of diffusion *p. 33*
  3. Process variables: a checklist *p. 38*
  4. Where change comes from *p. 41*

IV.   Characteristics of resisters and innovators *p. 45*

  1. Resistance *p. 45*
  2. The innovators *p. 51*

V.   Traits and functions of innovative institutions *p. 55*

VI.   Planning and executing change *p. 61*

  1. Overview of models *p. 61*
  2. Overview of strategies *p. 65*
  3. Three models of how change takes place *p. 70*
  4. Choice of models *p. 84*

VII.   Evaluating innovations. p. 85

VIII.   Summary and conclusions p. 91

Bibliography p. 95

Introduction

Only in fairly recent times have we come to look on change as something positive, as possibly better than continuity. Even today, in
a great many circles, educational change is suspect, as something
unproved and unusual, even indeed dangerous. To change education
amounts in fact to changing the way parents bring up their children.
It alters the relationships between adults and young people and
disturbs the controls the former have over the character of the
coming generation. It is hardly surprising, therefore, that educational ideas, habits and patterns normally change very slowly.
History shows, in fact, that education is a domain where there
has almost never been a radical rupture between the new and the
old.

The processes of assimilation (taking in new ideas or practices)
and accommodation (adapting former structures to these new ideas
or practices) are by their nature slow and gradual. The very notion
of innovation is in a sense a conservative one, in that its primary
function is to make the unfamiliar into the familiar, to graft the
new onto the old. In education, we are dealing with social institutions as well as the adults who work in them, and this strength-
ens still further the inbuilt resistance to change. Inevitably,
it seems, the quest for novelty must be subordinated to the desire
for stability.

The opposing view is the 'linear' theory of Spencer: that there
will always be steady progress towards improved schooling whether
or not we consciously plan to that end. One of the purposes of the
present study is to examine these propositions. Only in the very
recent past have social scientists begun to dissect the anatomy of
social change in order to find out why a certain type of modifica-
tion is more effective than another, why some changes spread rapidly and others slowly, what are the resistances to change in human
affairs and why particular strategies for changing institutions
succeed or fail. In the course of this study, we shall try to

answer some of these questions, and present evidence to help in the solution of others, as they apply to education.

The first three chapters deal with what change is, where it originates, how it is brought about, who is involved and in what context, where it happens and why it happens so infrequently. The second part examines the factors which determine whether and in what form changes can be introduced; the characteristics of innovators, innovative systems and resisters; the different ways of planning change, and the problem of evaluating innovations. We shall approach these questions both from the point of view of the people who are being changed (adopters, 'target public', teachers in an institutional context) and of those who are doing the changing, the so-called 'change agents'.

The vastness of the subject and the diversity of national cultures preclude any possibility of making blueprints or formulating laws describing how educational changes come about and how we can accelerate change. We must be content for the present to look closely at the elements aiding or hindering new developments in education, rather than attempt to design elaborate models of the process involved. There are four general points on which a great deal of work needs to be done in different cultural and political systems if we are to understand that process better.

1. There are ways of identifying and describing 'innovativeness' as it appears in individuals, in institutions and systems of education. We are beginning to understand how, in certain schools, change encourages and reinforces what is already in operation whereas, in others, it encounters resistance. We also know that school systems, like all human or 'open' systems, have a drive to maintain order and certainty and a countervailing drive to improve and innovate. It is these mechanisms which determine the response to innovation.

2. It is possible to predict whether and in what conditions an innovation will be accepted or resisted. Some of the principal variables are the complexity of the innovation, its cost, communicability, divisibility into parts, the nature of the relationship between the source of change and the persons being helped to change, and the congruence between the innovation and the environment.

3. Since the school system does not normally have the responsibility of evaluating its practices in order to see if changes are needed, most innovations come from outside. In consequence there can be no assurance that they will be adopted in more than a superficial manner. The most durable and effective innovations are those which the user has internalized; that is, which he has embraced because they satisfy his own specific needs. This implies that we should begin to use radically different methods of institutionalizing changes and using outside expertise.

4. The critical factor seems to be not the nature of the innovation nor its potential for improving learning, but rather the adopter's concept of the changes he personally will be required to make. Innovations in fact seem never to be installed for their intrinsic value. Whenever an important innovation is proposed teachers and administrators are being asked to interact differently with each other and with the students; hence the immediate emphasis must be on changing attitudes and only later on changing practices or procedures.

Like education itself, the process of change can only be understood with the aid of several separate disciplines. For example:

Anthropology: study of change arising from contact between cultures.

Sociology: social innovations (co-operative activities, patterns of household expenditure).

Rural sociology: spread of new farming practices and materials.

Mass communication: public opinion formation.

Social psychology: willingness to accept change (friendship and kinship factors, socialization, group dynamics).

Clinical psychology: personality change, behaviour change, counselling and therapy.

Market research: diffusion of new products.

Medical research: adoption of new drugs and of new practices in public health.

Unfortunately, there does not exist an elaborate theory of social change which would aid us in linking these different elements. In education, interdisciplinary groups of specialists have not yet found a common language, common methods of research and common perceptions which would allow them to converge on educational problems. Nonetheless, the literature on change in education has grown

3

steadily. Havelock [23], who has produced an encyclopedic volume on 'diffusion and utilization of knowledge' - i.e., how theoretical knowledge becomes practical knowledge - found less than 50 items dated before 1954, but some 500 annually by 1964. The literature covers curriculum change, organizational change, the development and spread of new educational ideas, practices, roles, materials and new organizational groupings. The 4,000 entries in Havelock's volume included a fairly large number of quantitative studies, but fewer theoretical studies and very few case histories.

Practically all Havelock's references are American. If we discount the anthropological literature on social change in primitive cultures, there seems indeed to be a near absence of non-American literature on change in education. Recently, some national studies have begun to appear in the publications of OECD and the Council of Europe, but the European literature still seems to be sparse, while in the developing countries the surface has barely been scratched.

The American literature on innovation in education has several limitations for our present purpose. Its language is often highly technical; it tends to look at change as an industrial process, i.e., a logical and rational development from theory to practice; it gives less emphasis to illogical types of resistance to change; it concentrates, like the British research in this field, on the behavioural aspects of change in 'roles' and interpersonal relationships; it often emphasizes and, perhaps, overrates, the importance of 'rewards' and 'reinforcement' of new habits in carrying out change. Finally, it has tended to neglect the importance of the social, historical and political framework in which all innovations operate.

It should be remembered that the Anglo-Saxon literature operates in a particular socio-cultural context. Therefore, the various models and strategies of change which we shall consider in this monograph reflect a limited cultural range. Clearly, the massive investment in research and development required in some of the American change models is inappropriate for the majority of countries. Similarly, the emphasis on intensive human relations training as a vehicle for accelerating attitude change in school personnel may be wholly out of place or even unacceptable in other cultures. Case studies from a number of different countries must be undertaken before we can examine more scientifically the process of educational change in an inter-cultural framework.

4

I Definitions : types, sources and processes of innovations

1. A WORKING DEFINITION: AN INNOVATION IS AN IMPROVEMENT WHICH IS MEASURABLE, DELIBERATE, DURABLE AND UNLIKELY TO OCCUR FREQUENTLY

As Westley [56] suggests, 'innovation' is a treacherous term, being both seductive and misleading: '... seductive because it connotes improvement and progress, when actually it only means something new and different. Misleading, because it displaces attention from the essence of the activity involved - learning - to a concern with the technology of education.'

This is well said. When educators write of 'change', they mean simply that something has happened between some original time, T_0 and some later time T_1, in the structure of the school system, in any of its processes, or in its goals or purposes. Putting bars on school windows or installing a language laboratory, for example, are equally involving 'something new and different'. Obviously, we must distinguish between innovations *per se* and innovations which are improvements. This raises the question of what constitutes an improvement in teaching or learning and how we are to measure whether the innovation was in fact the cause of the improvement.

For the present we can say that innovations (a) can only be assessed in relation to the objectives of an educational system, (b) are generally connected with increased or more individualized learning, more professionalized teaching and more refined curricula, and (c) involve a corresponding change in the activities and attitudes of school personnel. Thus, a new seating arrangement in one classroom and a major piece of national legislation are both innovations, though differing greatly in scale.

Here is a rather laborious but functional definition [44]:
> *Innovation is ... the creative selection, organization and utilization of human and material resources in new and unique ways which will result in the attainment of a higher level of achievement for the defined goals and objectives.*

5

A further clarification is needed. Do we mean by a change or innovation something which is entirely novel or rather something which is new from the standpoint of the persons using it? Schon [49] claims that an act is innovative only if it adds to the sum of known inventions. Otherwise, it is only a borrowing or a wider diffusion of the original act. In education, however, we are less concerned with the invention of new methods or devices than with their utilization and their dissemination throughout the school system. Most local changes are adaptations of something already practised in a neighbouring school. It is therefore the aspect of adoption that interests us, the fact that a student, teacher, administrator or entire school puts into operation a concept, attitude or tool which is qualitatively and measurably different from those which were used in the past. We are concerned, then, with the process whereby the new product is made available, is spread through the system and its integrated into other operating practices.

There is also a distinction between 'change' and 'innovation'. The latter is somehow more deliberate, willed and planned, rather than occurring spontaneously [35]. This is what Westley meant when he spoke of diverting attention from learning to a concern with technology. Innovation as a purposeful process brings us into the realm of social technology, the devising of the most effective combination of means to bring about specific ends. This is reflected in the preoccupation of international seminars with 'the management of education' and 'strategies of change' on the premise that change in education 'can no longer be left to casual initiatives by separate groups and persons' [11].

The implication is that innovation is a one-shot operation, with the objective of getting a given change installed, accepted and used. There are two points here. First, deliberate changes of this sort seem to take place infrequently, possibly because organizations prefer stability and seldom have mechanisms for change from within. Second, as education authorities become interested in innovation, more experiments will be tried, but the majority are likely to be discontinued. To come within our definition, an innovation must last, have a high rate of utilization and should resemble its intended form as planned. The educational system is too often prone to change in appearance as a substitute for change in substance.

6

2. GENERAL SOURCES OF CHANGE AND ENABLING FACTORS

If it is agreed that innovation is a positive force in education
and that planning is likely to increase the chances of its diffusion
and adoption, we must look briefly at the sources of change. How
are innovations designed and put into practice? What are the motives
or impulses to innovate? In what conditions are innovations more
likely to appear? These questions will be scrutinized later. Mean-
while, let us set out the general parameters.

What happens? One analyst [56] sees three processes at work.
(i) Innovations occur through the accretion of small changes:
introduction of a new textbook, better professional preparation of
teachers, newer testing and diagnostic methods. As in quantum theory, changes are generated slowly but amount to continual improvement in the system. (ii) The 'grass roots' theory: the system is
receiving new ideas all the time and transforming those it is
ready to assimilate into a new form in keeping with its own norms
and practice. (iii) Change through policy decision: nothing happens
within the educational system until a central governmental authority decides to adopt a new idea and issues the necessary executive
orders. All three processes are probably at work in most innovations.

What are the sources? In studying cultural change, anthropologists have developed a dichotomy between 'creative change' and
'deficit change'. This is really another version of the psycholo-
gist's distinction between tension-producing motives and tension-
reducing motives, but it may prove useful in classifying the
sources of change. By creative motives to innovate is meant a
voluntary and self-imposed desire to change customary usages, to
reduce the gap between the objectives of the system and present
practices, to redefine problems, to recognize new problems and to
create new ways of dealing with them. A number of ego psychologists claim that growth, change and development are motives inherent in every organism. According to several sociologists, they
are inherent in all groups and institutions as well. Put crudely,
the theory is that we have an innate need to upset our personal
and organizational equilibrium, to be curious and exploratory, to
correct unsatisfactory practices, to generate new ideas, to do
things we have never done.

Behind this notion may well lurk the American credo of change
for its own sake, echoes of which were heard at the recent OECD
workshop on the management of innovation in education [11].

The participants, at one point, were unable to determine what cons-
tituted negative and positive innovations. The seminar then deci-
ded that   'in a changing society, the capacity to adapt rapidly
and continuously to change was itself the desired quality... Innovation was by definition desirable and therefore people ought to
want change'. [54] Trow argues that innovation in higher education
comes less from a sense of inadequacy of existing arrangements
than from boredom with what one has been doing. Change is therefore a break with habit and routine, an obligation to think in
fresh ways about familiar subjects and reconsider old assumptions.
It is done primarily for its own sake and secondly for its outcomes.

Deficit motives to change, on the other hand, would be occasioned by crisis, competition or conflict: student or teacher
strikes, dissatisfaction of citizens at large or of national
officials, internal conflicts between administrators and teachers,
shortages of teachers or facilities, so-called 'educational emer-
gencies' such as the American reform of high-school science after
the launching of the first Soviet satellite.

Finally, there are a number of factors in the environment which
predispose educational systems to change. We shall be looking
later into more specific variables (e.g. size, complexity, finan-
ces, congruence between practices and values of receivers and the
innovation). At this point, some of the more general aspects of
the readiness for change may be mentioned. Miles [37] writes
of the cultural atmosphere or *Zeitgeist* in the United States which
creates specific pressures toward change and applies sanctions for
not changing. During these periods - generally ones of turbulence
or impending change in the social system - a 'family' of innovations develops and tends to stimulate others. Miles gives the example of 8 mm. sound film, which occurred in a setting of high interest in educational technology - programmed learning devices, educational TV, language laboratories.

Other pre-conditions may be listed: the fact that schools as
social institutions will change more rapidly during periods of general social changes; increasing public concern for quality education; increasing interest in technological advances; higher
allocations for research and development; greater affluence; growth
within the education system itself; the rising educational quali-
fications of parents and graduates; the growing proportion of the
gross national product devoted to formal education, etc.

8

There seem to be two principles at work. First, there is a 'critical mass' factor: the amount of new energy or the amount of pressure to change which is being generated relative to the total size of the system. This pressure from the environment obliges the educational system to change far more rapidly than under normal operating conditions. Secondly, there seems to be a 'critical threshold', similar to the take-off point in economic growth which is reached when a certain proportion of the national income is invested over and above the investment needed to maintain the population at the same standard of living. Applied to education, this concept requires that a certain percentage of time, personnel and finance be devoted to promotional activities (research development, experimentation) that transcend day-to-day operations, before a cumulative process of innovation is set in motion.

3. TYPES AND DEGREES OF CHANGE

What kinds of changes are in fact introduced into school systems? In general, they are of three sorts: 'hardware', that is additions to school equipment, such as new classrooms, teaching machines, books or playgrounds; 'software', usually in the content and range of the curriculum, or in the methods of delivery and reception; and as a sub-category of software 'interpersonal relations' - changes in the roles and relationships between teachers and students, between teachers and administrators or teachers and teachers (as in team teaching).

In education, changes in hardware imply changes in roles and relationships, since the 'product' of the school system is a human quality (children's learning), and the 'fabrication' of the product is primarily by interaction between adults and children. Lippit [28] points out that the innovation and spread of new teaching practices must therefore be a different process from the diffusion of new developments in agriculture, medicine and industry, where the innovation is usually a concrete article - a machine, seed, drug, insecticide. In education, most changes involve a different pattern of human behaviour, a different way of behaving towards a group of young learners. A farmer introducing a new machine need not be concerned with the 'attitude' of the soil or the seed. In education, however, most innovations bear directly on social relationships. The fact that educational operations are carried out by persons as instruments of change rather than through the use of physical technology (tools, machines, operating processes) makes it necessary to change basic attitudes when we change behaviours or skills.

9

If new tools are easier to introduce than changes in interpersonal relations, we can also say that an innovation requiring
individual acceptance (often called 'unencumbered knowledge') is
easier to install than one requiring group or widespread acceptance ('encumbered knowledge'). The introduction of a film projector as optional equipment for a teacher, for example, would
be simpler than the introduction of team teaching. This is another way of saying that 'things' or 'information' are easier to
cope with than changes in practice, attitudes or values. This
proposition is represented in a simple form in Fig. 1.

Fig. 1. Time and difficulty involved in making various changes

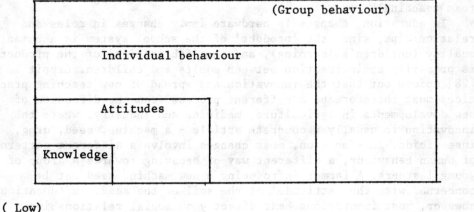

(High)

(Group behaviour)

Individual behaviour

Attitudes

Knowledge

(Low)

(Short) _____ Time involved _____ (Long)

In discussing types of change, a distinction must be made between how much change is required and what kind of changes are involved. Havelock divides the first category into four types [23].

(i) Change in size and scope of operations – requiring outlays of capital, labour, space and equipment.

(ii) Acquiring new skills – as in retraining teachers for new curricula, team teaching or the utilization of language laboratories.

(iii) Changing goals – as in the introduction of self-instructional materials, where the teacher becomes a non-directive helper rather than an authoritative conveyer of information.

(iv) Changing values or orientation – where many of the adopters' long-held principles are at stake, as in the elimination of examinations, school desegregation or the abandonment of religious instruction.

The second category, involving the type of change required for adoption or adaptation, may be of six sorts.

(i) Substitution – probably the most common and most readily accepted innovation, in which one item is substituted for another previously in use (a new textbook, new equipment in a science laboratory or, somewhat more complex, a replacement for a teacher or administrator).

(ii) Alteration – involving changes in existing structures rather than a complete substitution of parts or elements. To take two examples from Miles' compendium of case studies, *Innovation in education*, there could be an alteration in hardware, as in the shift from 16 mm. silent film to 8 mm. sound films, or a structural shift, as in a transfer of responsibilities for school guidance from senior teachers to a specialist. In both these cases, Miles noted that the innovations met with stiff resistance, either because the potential user found the proposal unfamiliar or because his status was affected.

(iii) Addition without changing old elements or patterns – those which can be added to an existing programme without seriously disturbing other parts of it (audio-visual aids, workshops, diagnostic tests).

(iv) Restructuring – seen either as a material rearrangement of work space (changing the composition and size of classes), rearrangements in the curriculum (introducing modern maths or a now foreign language) or as a revision of interpersonal relations (team teaching, para-professional teaching aids, non-graded schools).

(v) Eliminating old behaviour - as, for example, changing from a single textbook or method of discussion in class or human relations training for reducing mutual suspicion or hostility.

(vi) Reinforcing old behaviour - where it is a question of transmitting or adopting knowledge which reinforces what is already practised, as in most refresher courses for teachers.

The two main variables in estimating the difficulty or facility of making changes seem then to be the complexity of the operation itself and the degree or type of behaviour change required of the receiver. By way of a resumé, we reproduce the simplified chart of Miller [40] (Fig. 2).

Fig. 2. Length and complexity of different types of innovations

Number of participants required	*Types of innovation*	*Length of time required to implement the idea or programme*
(many)	Organizational (ungraded, team teaching)	
(several)	Instructional (ETV, new math, programming)	
(few)	Methodological (inductive teaching, new approach to reading)	

4. ENGINEERING EDUCATIONAL CHANGE

The very idea of planned change is a recent phenomenon in education.
Watson [55] has pointed out that most innovations are introduced:

    sporadically rather than continuously;

    by outside pressure rather than generated from within;

    for reasons of expediency, rather than as an expression of
    conviction or through deliberate planning;

    one here, one there, rather than in a cumulative and integrated
    design;

    much later than desirable, lagging rather than leading; super-
    ficially, rather than at a basic fundamental level;

    to win praise or promotion for certain individuals, rather than
    to improve educational performance.

The traditional role of social systems and institutions has
been to perpetuate the behaviour, morals and values of the society
in which they function. The idea of systematically planning technological change, of managing the process whereby theoretical knowledge becomes practical knowledge, is only some 100 years old, having started with the industrial research laboratories of the German
chemical industry in the late 19th century. Only within the past
half-century have industrialists, followed by social scientists,
tried to design an orderly system for converting human ability
and knowledge into goods or services with the object of modifying
existing patterns and institutions.

Schon [49] has constructed a three-stage model in which he
separates the least progressive from the most progressive industries.
In the craft stage, as illustrated by the ceramics and leather industries, change is made intuitively and empirically. In the mechanical ingenuity stage, in the auto industry, for example, changes
are made through a systematic investigation of current products and
methods with the object of improving them. At the third phase,
production and quality control, research in materials and processes
is carried out without any certainty of where the research will
lead. Promising discoveries are then referred to developments units
which design new products and processes. Schon places the chemical
and electronics industries at this level and notes that these industries were able to invade other markets (textiles, construction
and machine tooling) as a result of their more advanced research
and development.

It would be a useful exercise to determine the criteria by which we could place the education systems of various countries in one or another of these stages. Such criteria might include systematic examination of the teaching and learning process, amount of time, funds and personnel invested in research and development work, creation of mechanisms to bridge the gap between university research and school practice, etc.

If we followed this exercise far enough, we should probably be obliged to correlate economic development and educational development. The best systems would probably be found to resemble the industrial process of 'R&D' (research and development): conducting basic scientific inquiries ; investigating (educationally) oriented problems; collecting operational and planning data; inventing solutions to operating problems; engineering packages and programmes for (educational) use; testing and evaluating solutions and programmes [23].

The main criticisms of this model are that it is too naively 'professional-centred', that it violates educational reality, that it takes little account of pressures from the environment, that it views schools as objects to be manipulated and, finally, that it imposes western or technocratic values as international norms. We shall examine these points later.

5. INTRODUCTION TO PROCESS MODELS

The research and development approach has the merit of showing the change process in a logical progression from discovery to utilization. The process can also be portrayed as a sort of chain reaction. Fig. 3 is adopted from a chart used by Havelock [23].

As rational as this paradigm may be, it contains some assumptions which may not be borne out when we look more closely at how change takes place in education. Changes to date have not in fact been the result of a careful process of planning, nor has research necessarily preceded innovation. Generally, innovators have tried something out and then revised it. There is also a 'paternalistic' premise in such a model: that the best results are achieved by experts who pronounce what is good for the practitioners - planning for and doing something to them rather than collaborating with them.

Perhaps the theory-into-practice model is still too futuristic or utopian for our present purposes. As an historical formula

14

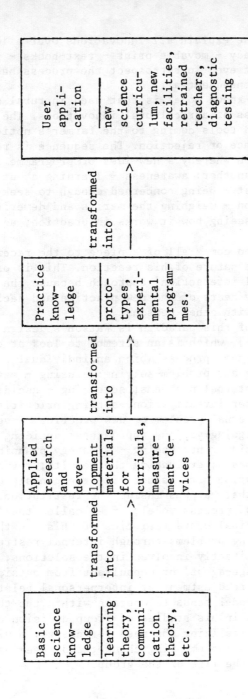

Fig. 3. Progress from basic research to application

Basic science knowledge		Applied research and development		Practice knowledge		User application
learning theory, communication theory, etc.	transformed into →	materials for curricula, measurement devices	transformed into →	prototypes, experimental programmes.	transformed into →	new science curriculum, new facilities, retrained teachers, diagnostic testing

it could of course explain all innovations over a long enough time span (e.g. literacy - movable print - text-books - programmed instruction), but even in retrospect the process has been neither deliberate nor consequential.

Another well-known model is that used in rural sociology to chart the progress of agricultural innovations. The focus is on new practices and tools coming to the farmer's notice and the syndrome of acceptance or rejection. The sequence is related to the cycle in education whereby a new idea or programme is adapted by one school from another: awareness - learning about the idea or practice; interest - being concerned enough to seek further information; evaluation - weighing the merits and demerits of the innovation; trial - seeing how it works in practice; adoption or rejection.

The innovation comes all of a piece to the receiver and the model follows the nature of his reaction. This is often referred to as the 'social interaction' approach because the potential adopter generally hears of the new practice and decides to use it by consultation with other persons.

A variation of this paradign is Watson's design for 'continuous self-renewal' [55], which is an attempt to look at change in organizations as the same process which an individual follows in constructive thinking and problem-solving: sensing - external trends and resources, internal problems; screening - deciding whether the items merit further investigation, setting priorities; diagnosing - analysing the internal problem or new practice; inventing - remedies, applications; weighing various approaches; deciding on a particular innovation or action; introducing - strategy planning; operating on an experimental basis; evaluating the results; revising.

The preoccupation here is not with the genesis of a new practice but rather with what happens inside the institution. This leads us to a third type of process model, often called the 'problem-solving model'. The principal characteristics of this are the following: emphasis on solving problems through internal restructuring, where the receiver is directly involved in the solutions; frequent use of a temporary 'change-agent' or consultant from outside; concern with attitude change, readjustment of interpersonal relations and communications. This model tends to operate within the three phases set out by Kurt Lewin in his studies of group decision and social change: unfreezing - realizing the need for change; moving - the activities involved in implementing change; and freezing - fixing the new behaviour in the life of the group.

16

In effect, two processes are at work. The first is one of
reeducation, the becoming aware of and correcting inefficient or
dysfunctional habits and attitudes; the second is properly educa-
tive, being designed to add new skills, knowledge, practices or
attitudes to a person or group [36].Viewed from within an organization, the sequence is as follows: criticism; changes proposed;
development and clarification of proposals; evaluation, review
and reformulation of proposals; comparison of proposals; action
to be taken on proposals; implementation of action decisions [33].

Viewed in the perspective of the change agent or consultant
coming into the organization (client system), we have the following
pattern: development of a need for change; establishment of a change
relationship between agent and client; clarification or diagnosis
of client system's problem; examination of alternative routes and
goals, establishing goals and action required; transformation of
intentions into actual change efforts; generalization and stabili-
zation of change; achieving a terminal relationship.

While we have no paradigm which consolidates these three process models into one, we can isolate the various components of each
and follow the interactions which take place between the invention
of a new idea or artifact and its ultimate use by practitioners,
as shown in Fig. 4.

Fig. 4. Interaction of agents involved in change [23]

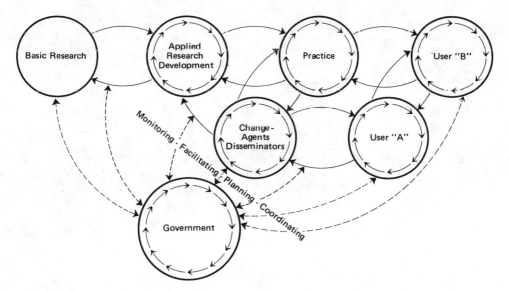

In a later section we shall look more closely at each of these models in order to determine in which type of education system they occur and how they are interrelated in the actual process of change. For the present it is important to note that the model will differ according to the concern with antecedents (the conditions prior to the introduction of the innovation), with the initiation and the incorporation of change, and with the evaluation of its effects. Different models also focus on different actors (the group, individual adopter, the teaching staff or administration, the developers, the opinion leaders or communicators) and on the relationship between the parties concerned.

II Individuals, groups, institutions, cultures : an overview of the agents involved in change

The units of analysis utilized by the various disciplines concerned with social change appear to be threefold: the individual as adopter (psychology, rural sociology, consumer research, public health), the group as key parameter (mass communications, social psychology, sociology), and the institutional and cultural framework (anthropology, political science). In any given educational innovation of importance, all three units are brought immediately into play. Teachers are placed in new relationships to materials, students or other teachers. Student-teacher-administrator-(parent) relations are changed. The school as a bureaucratic organization is modified, as are its relations with external institutions with which it is involved. Finally, since education is a microcosm of the culture which it embodies and transmits, changes in content (sex education, religious education) or method (non-directive teaching, group work) will reflect alterations in the surrounding environment.

In analysing the process of change, therefore, we must study a wide, complex range of variables operating in a highly integrated system: individual perceptions, group process norms, organizational structures, pressures from the community and ministry, cultural codes. One system of classifying these variables is by dividing them into participants, structures and roles or relationships: *Internal and external participants* [33]. The internal participants, those directly concerned with the legal or social system in education, include students, teachers, school principals or directors, supervisors or inspectors, local administrative directors (superintendent, head of public instruction, parents, legislatures, national or regional ministries, judicial authorities). The external participants, exerting indirect influence through dissemination of information, raising expectations or invoking sanctions, include non-educationists (public figures or opinion leaders), foundations or research councils, academics, industry and mass media (notably the textbook industry and other materials and

19

facilities producers), educationists active in professional organizations and certain branches of national government (labour ministry, military, social affairs).

Formal and informal structures [57]. The formal education system (ministries, inspectorate, local school system itself) is only a part of the education structure. Innovations must take into account ancillary structures and institutions. Ancillary structures are formally organized systems contributing to but not part of, the formal system: parent-teacher associations, textbook manufactures, school committees, mental health organizations, etc. The third type of structure is the autonomous group made up of individuals within the education system: friendship groups or cliques. The final type, institutions, is made up of in-school relationships which follow prescribed norms: informal rules of conduct, status differences among teachers and administrators, treatment of parents.

Classification by role and relationship: The school system is composed of interlocking positions and interacting roles. Each position (parent, school board member, superintendent, teacher, principal, student) requires a role performance in relation to other positions. As roles interact within the system and in response to larger systems (state, regional, national, international educational bodies), they change relationships. For example, those lower in the hierarchy of power and prestige adapt by conforming more than those at the higher levels [55]. The key relationships must be looked at to gauge the direction and effects of change: school director – board of education; school director – ministry; inspector – principal; principal – teachers; teacher – teacher; teacher – student; teacher – parent; superintendent – community power figure [39].

Another way of looking at the interactions taking place on different levels is by following the effects of a given innovation on the various agents. The linkage is shown in Fig. 5.

Individual change. That the introduction of audio-visual aids and programmed instruction has met with resistance on the part of teachers is an indication of how new tools and devices are immediately 'personalized' when they are proposed for educational purposes. Most educational improvements involve changes in what the teacher must know and do, which in teaching is closely related to the way a person conceives his professional identity. As values and attitudes are at stake in all mechanical-structural changes

20

Fig. 5: Linkage in the process of educational change

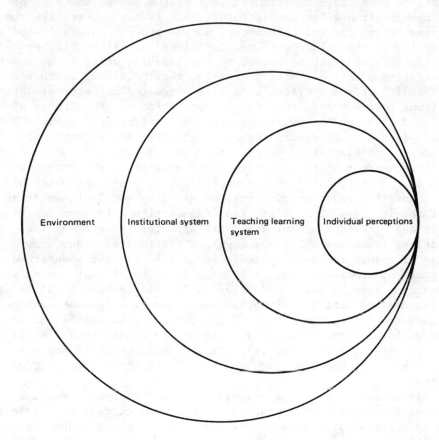

Environment   Institutional system   Teaching learning system   Individual perceptions

in education, personal attitudes — what psychologists call the
'self system' — inevitably come into play. The result on the
adopter is usually high anxiety, prolonged resistance and the
necessity of a much deeper involvement in 'unlearning' and 're-
learning' than is brought about by simply giving him written information about a new practice. As Schon [49] points out, we are
technologically but not emotionally an adaptive society. While we
encourage new inventions, we have not taken steps to facilitate
the necessary changes in attitude and behaviour which must
accompany them.

What are the practical implications for educational innovation?
First, we must judge the significance of the change in terms of
the meaning it has for the acceptor. That is not necessarily the
meaning it has for the introducer, as was brought out in Atwood's
study [2] of the guidance counsellor hired to relieve teachers of
additional duties but perceived by the teaching staff as a threat
to existing practices. More precisely, the individual teacher's
personality or value system is a less adequate indicator of his
attitude toward change than is his perception of the effects of
the innovation on his own interests and institutional goals. What
counts is the relative importance he attaches to the personal
avantages and disadvantages of each change.

This means that the planning and execution of the change process is a developmental, not a mechanical, process, in which both
the innovating and receiving systems are altered. Implementation
will require as much time as planning, particularly when teaching
roles and classroom organization are affected (programmed instruction, teamteaching, group work). Unfortunately, our knowledge of change in human systems lags far behind our understanding
of physical processes. Chin and Benne [12] insist that a massive
investment must be made in developing 'people technologies' before
we can deal effectively with the human aspects of planned change.
We know too little about how and why persons change their attitudes, about group behaviour and about the cognitive and skill
requirements of retraining teachers and administrators for the
new types of interaction required in a learning-oriented school
system.

All schools are living organizations and respond accordingly
to revised patterns of operation. Some of the current innovations
(independent study, ungraded classes, teacher aides, team teaching,
flexible scheduling, computer scheduling) require important adjust-
ments in the ways school personnel interact, apart from changes in
duration and regularity of their contact. One recent American
study [24] has shown that the 'innovativeness' of a given school
system can be measured by the type of interpersonal relationships
or norms percieved to exist in that system, e.g. the principal
as perceived by the professional staff, the type of interaction
among the professional teaching staff, the effectiveness of professional staff meetings in solving problems, etc. Certain types
of interpersonal relations or such concepts as 'openness' and
'trust', as measured in Q-sort or conventional attitude tests,
can maintain or create a psychological climate for change and innovation.

Organizational and evironmental changes. Whereas the teacher is the key figure in the final implementation of an innovation that bears directly on the learning process, he is much less significant in the organizational mechanism. As durable, permanent structures, schools outlast individual teachers. For the administrator, inspector and governmental official, schools are essentially bureaucracies, and the teacher is not a professional but a functionary. Few innovations can be introduced by teachers, despite their high degree of autonomy in the classroom. The moment that any change introduced by the teacher in the classroom touches on new space arrangements, instructional materials or equipment, new forms of testing or reporting students, the administrative machine is set in operation. The teacher ordinarily feels as helpless to influence the larger organizational structures as would a subordinate in any other public service.

The school, in turn, is closely linked to its environment: to the influence of parents, community organizations, ministerial directives, mass media, university departments of education and teacher-training institutes. As a highly vulnerable, visible and dependent community agency, the school can only make changes — assuming that the school initiates these changes, which is seldom the case — so long as they do not conflict with the community's concept of what education should be. Sex education and non-directive teaching methods, for example, are unlikely to take root in a community with morally rigid and authoritarian standards. All instructional programmes and practices are related to the process of 'socialization', the training of children in the values and habits of society, aided by the family and such institutions as the church. If instruction is based on authoritative presentation of a subject by the teacher and on its passive absorption by the student, it is incidentally a process of socialization to authoritarian relationships with adults. If, on the other hand, pupils are encouraged to discover principles for themselves through observation and inference and with less guidance from the teacher, this is a process of socialization to personal and intellectual autonomy [52].

It follows that we are unlikely to have a more developed school system in the sense of child-centered, 'non-directive' or highly individualized teaching, than the social context in which it is operating. We know that there are political, cultural and economic settings which discourage innovation, placing greater stress on education as a semi-religious activity and with a general hostility towards social and cultural change. Such communities place a high value on the past, often have low educational attainments, lack the specialized skills and training associated with modern technology and have few outside contacts with other communities. On the other hand, a community with 'modern' norms will have a more developed technology with a complex division of labour, will place a high value on experimentation in technical and social affairs, will have wider contacts and receive larger amounts of information from other communities.

There is thus a fairly close correlation between the rate of innovation, the economic level of a given country (as measured by GNP or by the customary list of human resource indicators) and the trend to non-directive instruction or more flexible classroom management. These criteria may tell us nothing about the quality of the education system nor about the appropriateness of the innovation; but they help us to predict the type and frequency of innovation for a given country or region. There are, however, schools of thought which definitely relate the quality of education to the type of instructional methods and so, indirectly, to the economic level of a country. Beeby [4] has designed a four-stage model for measuring the quality of primary education as it is related to teacher education. In the first stage, teaching activities are primitive or loosely organized. They often involve the transmission of symbols without meaning or memorization rituals on the part of pupils. In the second stage, classrooms are organized rigidly; teaching methods and examinations are highly standardized; there is frequent inspection by ministerial authorities. The third stage is characterized by greater initiative on the part of students and more flexibility in teaching practices. Finally, in the fourth stage, pupil problem-solving and self-initiated activity are common. Emotional as well as cognitive development becomes an important aim, as does the relationship between the teacher and individual students.

III System and process : the major variables

1. WHY SCHOOLS CHANGE SO SLOWLY

We have noted that education systems are more resistant to innovation than industrial or business enterprises, and that teachers are
more difficult to change than farmers or physicians. What are the
individual and institutional factors at play here, and how do they
function at various points in the change process?

As Miles has pointed out, permanent systems — whether persons,
groups or organizations — find it difficult to change themselves.
'The major portion of available energy goes to carrying out routine
operations and maintenance of existing relationships within the
system. Thus the fraction of energy left over for matters of diagnosis, planning, innovation, deliberate change and growth is ordinarily very small' [36]. All organizations tend to achieve, maintain
and return to a state of equilibrium, which is perhaps our way of
preserving our identity, character, institutions and cultures.
Brickell argues that institutional stability ensures that the institution produces the maximum results at a given moment. Any change
will automatically reduce production, at least until new habit
patterns are formed [6]. According to systems theory, social systems are stable and homeostatic; after minor disturbances they
return to a state of equilibrium resembling their previous state
[55]. This gives them a sort of self-regulating character allowing
them to meet the demands of the environment without being perma-
ently disturbed.

A number of behavioural scientists, applying this theory to
educational institutions, claim that schools are by nature stable
or homeostatic and are therefore unable to innovate. To test this
hypothesis, let us look at the genotypical and phenotypical characteristics that inhibit change. Havelock [23] divides these into
input factors, which inhibit change from entering into the school
system; output factors, which prevent the genesis of change from
within; and throughput factors, which limit the spread of new
ideas and practices through the school system.

25

Resistance to change from the environment. The community at large
does not usually encourage or expect change in the school system,
unless a crisis is detected in internal functioning. There is a
related belief, often sponsored by the teaching staff, that children are too fragile and valuable to be subjected to experimentation.

'Incompetence' of outside agents. Most parents and community
officials know too little about teaching or learning — or are
encouraged to think that they do — to judge any innovation that
is not an outright policy matter. This may also be true of the
majority of ministry officials who are not 'professionals', with
the possible exception of the inspector and chief administrator.

Overcentralization. Since most systems are large and centralized,
power is concentrated in the hands of a small number of senior
officials. This slows down drastically the rate of change, and
filters all efforts at innovation through a bureaucratic, rather
than professional agency.

Teacher defensiveness. Teachers are typical in resenting any
changes brought into the schools without their participation from
the beginning, or if the decisions are made by others than their
recognized superiors. In particular, the outside 'change agent' is
seen as a threat to the integrity of the system and often occasions
withdrawal into the ritualistic use of existing procedures. In general, school personnel are oversensitive to criticism, perhaps
because the school system, of all public institutions, is the most
open to criticism from the entire community.

Absence of change agent or 'linking pin'. In education, as in
agriculture or engineering, there is no recognized agent responsible
for bringing and demonstrating new practices directly to the
teacher or administrator. The agricultural extension worker brings
information, samples and demonstrations of new seeds or farming
practices directly to the farmer. The systems engineer in the American Telephone and Telegraph Company has the role of surveying the
entire system and its components (basic research, applied research,
development, manufacturing, service) and of relating each component to the needs and resources of other components [23].

The 'detail man' in medicine, who brings new drugs from pharmaceutical companies to physicians, has a somewhate similar function. In education, such an agent usually comes from the university or a research institute. He has infrequent contact with teachers; he must first pass through an administrative filter; he is usually not asked to come to the school, and his advice is seldom valued, unless he is or has been a school teacher or administrator.

Incomplete linkage between theory and practice. As mentioned earlier, educational research is still underdeveloped, and there is no direct way of getting research findings from the laboratory into the school and classroom. A good deal of this research is unrelated to practical problems and experimental conditions have little in common with the way in which classroom life goes on under normal circumstances. When teachers, administrators and researchers do not have their work linked by any institutionalized means, research and practice tend to operate in two different social systems, with few shared values, few common perceptions, different 'coding systems' for communicating and finally more insulated interests. Practitioners in the schools have a reduced 'knowledge base' about new practices or developments. As a result, in market economy countries, the system often falls prey to textbook and materials manufacturers or their salesmen.

Underdeveloped scientific base. Inventions in education do not have the proven validity of scientific inventions. Most learning theories are not yet highly developed: many are incompatible. New practices can seldom be justified on a scientific basis before being tried out, and they are seldom evaluated carefully. In particular, the exaggerated claims for a number of technological innovations have not been borne out.

Conservatism. The school has traditionally seen its role as one of resisting pressures from without. Socialization is principally a process of conservation, of assuring the cultural continuity rather than of provoking cultural change. Finally,changes in the environment are only incorporated into the school when they are fully stabilized.

Professional invisibility. The basic activity in the school-teaching — takes place out of sight of adult contact or supervision 90 per cent of the time [39]. As a result, it is hard to get correct information as to whether in fact teaching and learning activities are in need of change. Children themselves are not normally allowed to comment on the teacher's performance and they have few sanctions to apply. For that matter, criteria for judging teacher effectiveness usually depend on the scale of values of a particular inspector or chief administrator.

Output factors.

Confused goals. There are two aspects to this problem: the contradictory goals within the school system and the fact that different members (teachers, administrators, parents, educators) stress one set rather than another — and thereby support certain changes while combatting others. In relation to the first aspect, Miles [39] puts it well:

> Since the public schools are supposed to bring about desirable changes in children and exist in an environment of so-called 'local control' amid a host of other subsystems, all with expectations for the school, educational goals are usually (a) vaguely staged; (b) multiple in nature, since the school is expected to do many different things to meet the wishes of its many publics; and (c) conflictful, in the sense that different publics may want mutually incompatible things. For example, the school is expected to cause children to 'achieve' mastery of academic subject matter and to develop and maintain physical and emotional health in children and to socialize children into industrial society (e.g. make them neat, obedient, prompt, achievement-oriented). There are many circumstances under which these goals may prove mutually incompatible.

There is the same ambiguity within the school system. School authorities may support or initiate changes aimed to produce an imaginative, co-operative, self-directed child (group work, self-instruction, non-directive teaching techniques), while the teaching staff prizes obedience, regularity, self-discipline. Also curricular changes, notably sex education or human relations training, are resisted on the premise that they lie outside the province of the school and are rather the responsibility of parents.

No rewards for innovating. Teachers, and to a lesser extent administrators, are not rewarded for initiating or carrying through innovations. Rather, they are rewarded for stable, dependable behaviour. Those adopting change are paid the same as those rejecting it and they run the added risk of possible failure. Promotions are generally made on the basis of seniority, personal influence, popularity or professional upgrading at the university. It has frequently been observed that 'rocking the boat' seldom pays in an organization.

Uniformity of approach. With such a diversity of backgrounds, aptitudes and motivation on the part of both students and teachers, the school seeks to install methods and procedures applicable to the greatest number. Innovations giving advantage to gifted or deprived children, to child-centred or subject-matter-centred teachers, to charismatic or bureaucratic administrators, are resisted by one party or the other.

School as a monopoly. Since schools do not have an economic motive nor face competition — apart from a quite separate network of private or denominational schools — they need be less concerned with improvement of their services. Parents who are dissatisfied may move to another district, but the school is not thereby threatened. Reichart [43] notes that the school is in the unique position of 'having been created as a monopoly by society to do what society has mandated'. Clients are not free to accept or reject the services of an obligatory education system. As a result, schools are 'domesticated' institutions, that is to say, their organizational environment is more stable than that of other types of institutions.

Low knowledge component — low investment in R & D. For an institution whose central task is the dissemination of knowledge, there is little investment in knowledge-acquisition or dissemination within the school itself. There is a limited awareness and little direct use of relevant areas of knowledge (learning psychology, social psychology, sociology of the community). Under-utilization of knowledge may be due in part to the fact that policy decisions are made by a board or lay persons rather than by professionals [39].

Miles [39] estimates that out of 30,000 school districts in the United States, there are only 100 which have a built-in research function, and most of these tend to become no more than administrative data-collecting and book-keeping devices. Only a dozen have a specific unit set up to develop new practices, test them for feasibility and efficacy, and diffuse them to other parts of the system.

Low technological and financial investment. The amount of technology per worker in schools is relatively low. From 70 to 90 per cent of the budget ordinarily goes to salaries, with a fraction for equipment and materials. The consequence is that social transactions, rather than socio-technical transactions, come to be the major working technique [38]. Sussman says: 'A school system which must house pupils in old, unsafe buildings, which can barely supply them with the minimum necessities in terms of textbooks, paper and chalk, which has a shortage of teachers — not to speak of specialists like testers and remedial reading staff — can hardly be expected to innovate. Even if an innovation promises to save money eventually, the process of instituting it is likely to be expensive'. The author also recalls Galbraith's observation that market economy countries have a tendency to affluence in the private sector and to underspending in the public sector.

Difficulty in diagnosing weaknesses. As the school is defensive towards external criticism and as teachers claim full autonomy to manage their classrooms, the diagnosis of weakness — normally the pre-condition of change — is retarded or stifled. Neither the school as a whole nor any of its personnel is rewarded for admitting that changes are needed.

Product measurement problems. It is difficult to identify the product of educational organizations. Many of the results are delayed over a long span of time. This difficulty can be used as an organizational defence against external criticism - in particular against criticism of the effectiveness of teaching practices. The stated goals being vague, multiple, conflicting and emotionally laden (children are valuable property) [39], why should teachers change their practices if it cannot be proved that one method achieves better results than another?

30

Experience shows that, within the narrow limits where exact
measurement is possible, it can be a stimulus to change. This has
been so, for example, with two of the criteria of output measurement ordinarily used, rate of pupil retention and financial investment per child.

Focus on present commitments — accountability. Few teachers, administrators or specialists are sufficiently detached from normal
operations to probe weaknesses or learn about promising practices.
Administrators are generally overburdened; teachers are responsible
for fixed numbers of students in fixed periods, with little time
for creative work.

Low personnel development investment. Little money is spent by
school systems on the development of personnel. Continuing education is regarded as an individual matter. Yet experience has
shown that major innovations in school systems only come about as
a result of personnel development efforts, often with outside funds
and facilities [39].

Lack of entrepreneurial models. The school system is not usually a
place where one finds individuals who sense needs, develop practices suited to meet those needs, and push them through the organization. Most school administrators are former teachers themselves,
and have built up too many personal allegiances within the system
to disturb the persons and groups who serve under them. At the
same time, for many reasons, of which several have been mentioned,
teachers are rarely innovators, particularly in highly developed
countries. They can seldom change any practice that extends beyond
their classroom and indeed are not expected to do so. As most
school systems are hierarchies, changes come from above; they do
not emerge at the work place. Hence, unlike most workers, teachers
seldom suggest new working patterns for themselves. Indeed, they
often see it as a reflection on their personal adequacy when they
are asked to imitate other teachers' methods.

Nor is the teacher generally an innovative character. Most
personality inventories in North American and European countries
depict teachers as restrained and deferent, lacking in social
boldness, anxious to please, more passive and less competitive
than professionals in other jobs. There is evidence that this
portrait is not exact in many developing countries.

Passivity. To cite Miles [39]: 'In many school systems, the main stance of the chief administrator in the face of system vulnerability and varying demands from the environment is a withdrawing, passive one ... The tacit view of the school is that it has little power to initiate, develop, grow, push things, or be disagreeable to anyone or anything.'

Throughput factors

Separation of members and units. The different parts of school systems are not as closely interlocking as those of industrial firms or other systems that produce and market physical objects. Miles [39] claims that a low degree of interdependence makes a system much more difficult to alter, since changes occurring in one part are not transmitted to another parts. Thus, the failure or success of one teacher has little impact on the teacher in the adjoining room. This low level of co-ordination constricts the flow of information about new thought and practice.

Education differs in this respect from other institutions where the innovation process has been researched. Farmers and physicians, for example, discuss new ideas and imitate one another, whereas there seems to be little interpersonal communication among teachers that leads to innovation.

Hierarchy and differential status. Most professional organizations have a higher rate of innovation than bureaucratic organizations, owing to the stress on expertise rather than rank, to the greater flexibility of members, to the more precise goals and output criteria, and to high demands for production. The Burns and Stalker study of industry [23] showed that several organizations were all but immobilized by their stress on the hierarchical status system and by the accompanying resistance of members to changing the structure.

In particular, hierarchies discourage or distort information flow. Members hesitate to send knowledge upward unless: (a) it is firmly substantiated by hard data, which can seldom be the case with innovations; (b) it reflects only a favourable evaluation of themselves; and (c) it is directly relevant to the receiver [23] .

The school structure has a more stultifying effect on initiation than on adoption of an innovation. In an authoritative system, anyone can be ordered to adopt something new but no one can be ordered to create something new. Enforced adoption, however, is likely to

32

be superficial and instable — an act of compliance rather than of
identification or internalization [23].

Lack of procedures and training for change. Teachers have no
institutionalized procedures for learning about the new practices
of colleagues. As mentioned earlier, there is also resistance to
adopting another teacher's ideas. Moreover, school personnel do
not enjoy the type of human relations training used in industry
and commerce to stimulate awareness and gain acceptance of new
ideas and methods.

2. CURVES AND RATES OF DIFFUSION

Appollonius of Perga discovered conic sections some 2,000 years
before they were applied to engineering problems. It took some
500 years for medicine to imitate Paracelsus by systematically
using ether as an anaesthetic. The first patent for a typewriter
was deposed in Great Britain in 1714; a typewriter was commercial-
ly available only 50 years later [53]. Since then, the length
of time required for the adoption of an innovation has been short-
ened as a general rule. Lynn's study of 20 major innovations —
including frozen food, antibiotics and integrated circuits —
revealed that the average time needed for a major scientific discovery to be translated into a usable form has been reduced by 60
per cent since the beginning of the present century [53]. The
most dramatic example was the explosion of the atomic bomb at
Hiroshima six years after the first experiments with nuclear fis-
sion.

The implementation rates in educational systems, however, still
lag behind those of industrial, agricultural or medical systems.
Of the many reasons already noted, Miles [37] isolates three:
absence of valid scientific research findings; lack of change
agents to promote new educational ideas; lack of economic incentive
to adopt innovations. According to Mort, change in the American
school system takes 'an extravagantly long time' and follows a
predictable pattern. Between the time in which there is recognition
of a need (example: identification of school children's health
problems) and the first introduction of a way of meeting the need
which eventually spreads throughout the system (example: health
inspection by a school doctor), there is a 50-year time lapse.
Another 50 years is required for diffusion or full adaptation.

During this second phase, it takes 15 years for the practice to appear in 3 per cent of the systems in the country. Thereafter, there is a period of 20 years of rapid diffusion, followed by a final 15 years of slow diffusion through the last small percentage of schools [41].

The rate of change in education has greatly accelerated since Mort's studies were made in the 1930s. Mort himself estimates an increase in tempo of 20 per cent. Coombs mentions a recent American survey in which, out of 27 innovations studied, 6 had been generally adopted in school systems throughout the country in 10 years [13]. In 1953, Mort [41] claimed that an outpouring of important new designs in education can soon be expected. 'These designs will spring from the combination of hundreds of innovations which have been stimulated during the past half-century by new insights into educational psychology and social change'. In particular, Mort argues that the major discovery made at the turn of the century — that the theory of formal disciplines is untenable — will lead to a long period of adjustment characterized by thousands of innovations which later in the century will merge into new concepts or designs.

We have already mentioned the fact that adoption occurs in stages. From Mort and from research in agriculture, we can plot the adoption process in an S-curve (Fig. 6). There is an early stage, when the 2 or 3 per cent of *innovators* decide to introduce the new idea; a second stage, in which the *early adopters* (about 5 per cent follow, having observed that there are no unfortunate results; a middle stage, in which the *majority* adopts quickly, influenced primarily by the innovators; and a late stage, when the small residue of resistors or *laggards* at least gives in. Finally, lying above the curve, is a small group that *never* gives in [23].

Fig. 6: Adoption of a cumulative curve

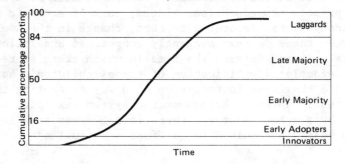

Havelock [23] makes the point that where a single adopter is concerned the progression from awareness to integration can be looked at as a similar learning curve, as shown in Fig. 7.

Fig. 7: Involvement of an individual during the adoption process

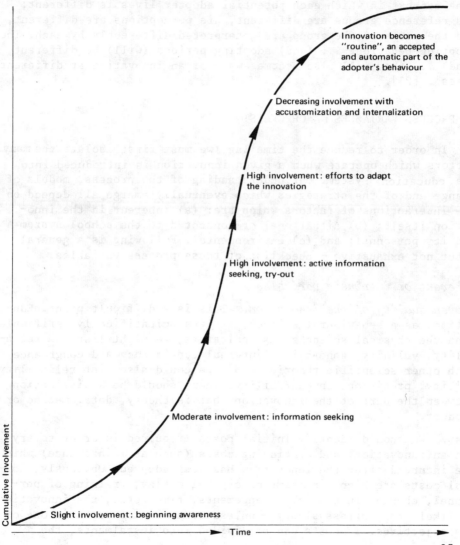

Innovation becomes "routine", an accepted and automatic part of the adopter's behaviour

Decreasing involvement with accustomization and internalization

High involvement: efforts to adapt the innovation

High involvement: active information seeking, try-out

Moderate involvement: information seeking

Slight involvement: beginning awareness

Cumulative Involvement

Time

In educational change we are generally concerned with a group, or at least with an accumulation of adoptions by individuals. Individuals are influenced by groups, so that diffusion curves look like chain reactions, with the number of adopters increasing in proportion to the number who have previously adopted [9]. At the same time, the adopting system affects each adopter differently. 'The context in which each potential adopter lives is different; his reference groups are different, his perceptions are different, and the norms of the group are interpreted differently by each. Their adopting behaviour ... (and) adopting periods (will) be different, (and) ... they will also become aware of an innovation at different times'. [23].

3. PROCESS VARIABLES : A CHECKLIST

In order to reduce the time lag, we must first isolate the many factors which operate when a given innovation is introduced into the education system. Our understanding of the process, models of change and of the strategies which eventually emerge all depend on the interactions of factors which are: (a) inherent in the innovation itself; (b) situational or connected to the school system and its personnel; and (c) environmental. Following is a general — but not exhaustive — checklist of these process variables.

Inherent or intrinsic variables

Proven quality of the innovation. This is a difficult point. Education, as a behavioural science, is less scientifically verifiable than the physical sciences. As indicators, we might list the reliability, validity, generality, internal consistency and congruence with other scientific theories [23]. We could also list reliability, utility, precision, and durability. There should be a distinction between the part ot the innovation that is theory, data, method or product.

Cost. We should identify initial costs (required in order to try out an innovation) and continuing costs (such as maintenance) which are incurred after the innovation has been adopted. Obviously, initial costs are high, in terms of capital outlay, training of personnel, changes in spatial arrangements, time, etc., the innovation is likely to progress slowly — unless reduction of costs is one of its objectives. If costs can be divided into instalments, the

36

obstacle is less serious. Havelock [23] notes that continuing
costs may not hinder the adoption of many innovations, since they
are likely to be underrated by the adopter at the time of adoption.

Divisibility. Havelock and Rogers [46] define this variable as
'the degree to which an innovation may be tried on a limited basis'. Innovations which meet this condition (adopted on a small
scale or for a limited period on a trial basis) are more readily
diffused than those which are an all-or-none proposition. School
buildings, computer terminals, open admission policies can seldom
be discontinued once delivered. 'This principle also holds in
industry. The probability that a firm will introduce a new technique of production is, in part, a function of the size of the
investment required' [23].

Divisibility can also refer to the number of individuals or
the proportion of a community to be involved in the adoption. Thus,
group consent means a slower diffusion than individual consent.
In MacKenzie's studies of curricular change, divisibility and cost
are linked: some changes involved employment of new staff (e.g.,
the teaching of Spanish). Some involved the use of a national
agency for retraining, as in the case of the newer maths content.
Others involved extensive local staff retraining, as in the case
of team teaching [33].

Complexity. This attribute refers to (a) the number of parts of
the innovation, (b) the number of behaviours or skills to be learned
or understood before adoption is possible, or (c) the number of
procedures required for effective maintenance over time [23]. The
more difficult it is to understand and use, the less rapidly an
innovation will be adopted. Earlier we spoke of the amount of
change required (changing size and scope of operations, acquiring
new skills, changing goals, changing values) and the type of change
(reinforcing old behaviour, substitution, addition without changing
former patterns, eliminating old behaviour, alteration, restructuring). Both can be plotted along a continuum from facility to
difficulty: things are easier to change than values, innovations
calling for a shift in well-formed habits of work and thought
being the most difficult to adopt. 'For example, if the innovation
absolutely requires that the progress of each child be noted every
day and that a new instructional decision be made specifically for
him, teachers may find this too much of a break from the mass instruction to which they are accustomed.' [7]

Communicability. How easy or difficult is it to explain or demonstrate the innovation? Anthropologists have found that material
items find more acceptance than ideas because their utility is more
easily demonstrable and because the items themselves are more visible. Thus, new reading materials diffuse more rapidly than new
methods of how to teach reading. Teachers in particular want to
observe new ideas, techniques or devices at work in actual classrooms under normal conditions. In the American reform of curriculum
in physics (PSSC), for example, it was found that the syllabus was
not widely adopted in regions where special institutes were held
but rather in the vicinity of the demonstration classrooms, where
neighbouring teachers could watch the programme for themselves.

A number of educational technologists claim that new materials
must be all but self-teaching if they are to be adopted. The more
readily they fit the demands of teaching situations and the more
easily they can be reproduced and distributed, without changing
their original form when used by a wide variety of teachers in
different situations, the more likely are they to be adopted. On
the other hand, the more difficult they are to operate (i.e., requiring extra administrative energy), or are puzzling or threat-
ening in a technical sense to the adopter, the more slowly will
they be accepted [37]. In schools where teachers are accustomed
to making their own materials, however, as is often the case in
developing countries, they might object to 'packages' which cannot
be modified by their own inventiveness.

Situational variables

Structure of the instructional system. Any number of factors can
be isolated here; following are but a few. Size — the largest and
smallest school systems are the most difficult to change, since
both institutional mass and tight cohesion are highly resistant
forces. Hierarchical institutions initiate change more slowly
but adopt change more rapidly (if often superficially) than
decentralized institutions. The key factor in a hierarchical
structure is the amount of dependence on authority felt by the
potential acceptor. A number of industrial studies show that the
tenure of the chief administrator is important. The number of innovations seems to be inversely proportional to tenure, on the premise that the longer he is in office, the less likely he is to
introduce changes. Financial resources are obviously crucial in
implementing change. Communities giving higher financial support

38

tend to have more innovative schools, perhaps because of the higher levels of education and occupation of the members.

Leadership and sponsorship. It is important to specify the nature of the relationship between the sponsor of the change and the persons being helped to change. The power relationship is clearly a key factor (the more powerful the sponsor, the more likely the adoption by others), as is the prestige of the sponsor or of the first persons to adopt. Mass media research dwells on so-called 'opinion-leaders' who exert influence on voting behaviour or adoption of new farming practices. These are persons who get new information around (communicators) or who are more influential in persuading others to adopt new practices (legitimators).

School environment. Although an indistinct factor, the institutional climate in which a specific innovation is to be introduced can be measured. Personnel attitudes, views of the proposal as a threat or a panacea, familiarities with changes of the same sort, can determine whether the climate is favourable, neutral or inhibiting. A special case is that of change occasioned by crisis. Crises tend to loosen structures and value systems and, thereby, speed the rate of adoption or at least weaken the force of resistance. Such changes, however, tend to be temporary, unless the organization is affected long enough for new patterns to take root. A number of social psychologists believe that when institutional crises can be provoked and guided, there will ensue a process of growth and development, much as in the case of an individual crisis.

Group norms. Depending on which target group is most affected by the proposed change — teachers, students, administrators, parents — the probable reaction of existing reference groups, clique structures and vested interests can be predicted. In particular, group norms concerning value placed on security and on assumption of risks should be examined in this connexion.

Personal characteristics of adopters. We shall speak of the traits of innovators in the next section. Adopters probably differ little from innovators except perhaps in being more prone to conformity, deference to authority, insecurity, etc. We should examine such factors as: age (younger persons being generally more flexible); education (positively related to 'innovativeness'); income and socio-economic status (also positively related); capacity to discriminate; ability to deal with abstractions; rationality; positive attitudes towards the profession. The key factor, however, is compatibility: the degree to which an innovation is consistent with the existing values and past experiences of the adopter [46]. As attitudes and self-perceptions may count more than individual traits, adoption rates depend on how closely the proposed innovation fits the experience, social and cultural values and physical environment of the individual or, as we shall see, the group.

Rewards and punishments. The profitability of an innovation can be judged from the point of view of educational quality, administrative efficacity, psychological satisfaction of teachers or students, etc. Once again, however, what matters is what the potential adopter thinks he stands to gain from adopting. When actual rewards (financial gain, advancement) and punishments (financial loss, demotion) are involved, they can also contribute to acceptance on a short-term basis.

Environmental variables

Innovation system congruence. The willingness of the community to support specific innovations depends on cultural values. Sex education, open discussions on religion, self-management in the classroom are all examples of innovations which will not be tolerated in schools if they are not tolerated outside. Conversely, we have had cases — the comprehensive school and local control, for example — in which the teaching staff in a number of countries was opposed to progressive reforms endorsed by the general public.

Culture is a sort of filter which rejects certain changes and brings about modifications in those that pass through. Anthropologists have shown that responses to change can only be predicted through a very careful 'consumer research' on the receiving environment. In studying the response of American Indians to Christianity, for example, it turned out that patrilineally organized tribes were more receptive than matrilineally organized tribes by virtue of the patrilineal symbolism of Christianity. The practice of boiling drinking water has been resisted where theories of 'hot' and 'cold' pervade ideologies of food and health. Television was adopted early by families who were more attuned to the present than to the past or future, etc. [27]. There are cultures — and schools — which resist borrowing or adapting from others, because they base their behaviour on spiritual rather than biological or empirical standards (e.g., seed for farming comes from a sacred store and cannot be substituted; child-rearing is ritualized according to religious script). Clearly, much more is at stake here than the details of the innovation itself. Countries are at many different levels with respect to the general appropriateness of change, as measured by various indicators. The stronger the cultural cohesiveness and hence the influence of neighbourhood and kinship groups, the slower will be the acceptance of new ideas and practices. Biased as it is, the distinction between traditional and modern societies is a good indication of how rapidly change is generated and incorporated under normal conditions. Such characteristics as the extended family system, class structure based on traditional social status, religious amd ethical values emphasizing duty or obedience rather than initiative and rationality — all tend to perpetuate an education system based on memorization, ritualization, fixed status, discipline-centred methods, verbalism, social prejudice. To measure this factor, rural sociologists simply tally the proportion of recommended farm practices adopted over a given mumber of years in a sample of countries.

Readiness. We spoke earlier of a 'critical mass' or a *Zeitgeist* which prepares the climate for adoption of a particular innovation. Perhaps the best way of measuring this variable would be (a) estimating the weight of public demand or (b) analysing the properties which the innovation has in common with other changes which already have been accepted. It is almost impossible to know where an innovation starts; it is already present in the target environment in other patterns. Self-instructional methods, student self-management, new curricula in art and music, non-graded classes can only take root in a school system that has become as concerned with individual students as with socialization, or in schools acting on motivational theories that students learn for other reasons than to avoid punishments.

4. WHERE CHANGE COMES FROM

Case studies of change in education, generally demonstrate that the initiative comes from outside the educational institution. School systems are more preoccupied with the operation of the existing programme, in keeping with the organizational tendency to

41

stability. Griffiths [18] maintains that changes made in response to insiders are concerned more with clarification of rules and internal procedures, while those made in response to outside are concerned with new rules and procedures, and possibly with changes in general purpose and direction. He also argues that practical administrators show they are well aware of this when they have recourse to external agents — consultants, evaluation teams, citizens' committees and professional organizations — to suggest and make changes.

Griffith's second proposition is the following: 'The degree and duration of change is directly proportional to the intensity of the stimulus from the supra-system'. Thus the events of May 1968 in France or the launching of the first Russian Sputnik (claimed to have doubled the rate of instructional innovation in New York in 15 months) would constitute crises accelerating the invention and adoption of change. For all that, the diffusion and durability of these changes is doubtful. No doubt a good deal of legislation was activated and much creative work undertaken in both cases. People — particularly people in the educational profession — change their habits slowly and defend them tenaciously. In the case of the Sputnik, Brickell [6] reports that despite the increased rate of curricular change (foreign languages, mathematics, science), the great majority of schools was untouched. 'Most changes involved an alteration in subject content (ordinarily different information and more of it), or in the grouping of pupils (most commonly class size reduced or varied). Few programmes embodied changes in the kind of people employed, in the way they were organized to work with students, in the nature of instructional materials they used, or in the times and places at which they taught. The programmes which did embody such changes often touched the work of only two or three teachers.'

Recent attempts to introduce change have been made by importing outside consultants. Two American projects to which we shall return, COPED and Research for Better Schools, used the 'trainer' or 'change agent team' as an instrument for internal reform. Miles [36] calls these mechanisms 'temporary systems'; they are, he says, more flexible, short-term 'task forces', as opposed to the 'permanent system' from which the school cannot escape. The most effective agents, both in industry and education, seem to be social psychologists who, as behavioural engineers, elicit the awareness of needs, problems, potential or new ideas from the 'client' himself, rather than originate new devices outright and then persuade consumers to adopt them. Many of the organizational procedures (role playing, sensitivity training, intensive conferences) are akin to counselling and psycho-therapeutic techniques used with individuals. Another technique is the assignemnt of a presumably neutral officer as 'dean of innovation and change' or 'roving educational catalyst' or vice-president for heresy'.

In market economy countries change is often expedited by commercial firms. A new textbook, for example, has immediate repercussions over a wide area. In the case of textbooks, audio-visual aids, laboratory materials or kits, profit-making firms tend to innovate early, before the majority of schools have begun to change, and to attack aggressively with advertising and sales representatives. On the other hand, commercial interests tend to obstruct changes which would reduce the market for a product already in use. The net result is that the more conservative schools are pulled forward and the more innovative are held back [6].

In a remarkable number of case studies, the decisive figure emerges as the chief administrator of the school or of the local education system. Employment of new teachers, addition of new courses, reallocation of time between different subjects, institution of experimental programmes: all tend to be applied from above. Perhaps this means simply that the external pressures through which most changes come are transmitted via the administrator, and that such changes are, after all, made essentially to please or placate outside agents.

However, the chief administrator is neither inside nor outside the system. He stands between the functionaries of the system and the representatives of the community and, as such, has a 'balancing role'.

Spindler [50] claims that for this reason 'school administrators are rarely outspoken protagonists of a consistent and vigorously profiled point of view. Given the nature of our culture and social system, and the close connexion between the public and schools, he cannot alienate significant segments of that public and stay in business'.

Whether the administrator can effect changes within the system depends on whether the nature of the system (hierarchical or decentralized) suits his leadership style (authoritarian, benevolent autocrat, charismatic leader, democratic leader). In an authoririan system, where teachers are accustomed to receiving detailed instructions, a *laisser-faire* attitude to change will evoke little response. One study shows that the principal's influence on the adoption of changes increases with the frequency with which he is seen engaged in offering constructive suggestions to teachers, bringing educational literature to their attention, talking to them about their personal and professional activities, or showing that he knows what was going on in a classroom [40]. Other studies show a high correlation between the amount of staff inventiveness, as measured by the mean number of new practices developed by each teacher, and the staff's awareness of the principal's support for innovative teaching.

IV Characteristics of resisters and innovators

1. RESISTANCE

Anthropologists maintain that resistance to change is proportional
to the amount of change required in the receiving system.
Psychologists note that individuals resist most strongly at the
point where the pressure of change is greatest. The change comes
to be perceived as a threat, and the individual reacts defensively,
often by using former practices more secretly. Havelock [23] reports
on an industrial study in which there was little disturbance or
resistance to change until the change was imminent. As a tentavive
hypothesis, we might say that teachers resist in particular all
changes which leave them with less control over the classroom or
over the students in it.

Most strategies concentrate on facilitating change by lowering
resistance. To take an example given by Watson [55], instead of
trying to persuade teachers to pay attention to individual differences among students, they should be invited to analyse the factors which prevent such attention (large classes, single textbooks,
standard tests). By removing these pressures, there is released in
the teacher a natural tendency to adapt to individual pupils in a
new form. Basically the technique is that of introducing innovation
by steps which are calculated to cause the least amount of resistance and disruption.

We can also look at resistance in terms of curves (a resistance
curve, which is the mirror image of an adoption curve) or in a
formula, where Innovation = Demand — Resistance [23]. Watson [55]
has set out a stage theory of resistance to typical innovations:

(i)   Massive, undifferentiated: few take the change seriously.

(ii)   Pro and con sides identifiable: resistance can be defined,
its power appraised.

(iii) Direct conflict: resistance is mobilized (this is the crucial stage).

(iv) The Changers in power: wisdom is needed at this stage to keep latent opposition from mobilizing. Resisters are now pictured as cranks, nuisances.

(v) The first circle: old adversaries are as few and alienated as advocates were in the first stage. Advocates now resist new change.

Resistance in personality

This topic is well covered in clinical literature, it is important to locate the mainsprings of resistance to change. Let us look briefly at the three taxonomies in the literature on innovation:

(a) Watson [55]: '8 forces of resistance'

(i) *Homeostasis*. The organic desire to maintain balance, expressed physiologically for example by the need to maintain fairly constant such states as temperature or blood sugar. Example: the school administrator who, after a short period of sensitivity training, is temporarily more open and receptive to suggestions from teachers, but soon reverts to his more characteristic brusque and arbitrary manner.

(ii) *Habit*. Unless the situation changes noticeably, organisms will continue to respond in their accustomed way. The familiar is preferred.

(iii) *Primacy*. The way in which the organism first successfully copes with a situation sets a pattern which tends to persist. Example: teachers who, despite in-service courses and supervision, continue to teach as they themselves were taught in childhood.

(iv) *Selective perception and retention*. Admitting only such new ideas as fit an established outlook, as in protecting prejudice by blocking out new information ... 'there's none so blind as those who won't see'.

(v) *Dependence*. Notably, on views of peers and hierarchical superiors.

(vi) *Superego*. The enforcement of moral standards acquired in childhood from authoritative adults. Example: blind respect for tradition.

(vii) *Self-distrust*. Example: hesitations on the part of students, parents, teachers and administrators to correct existing mal-practices.

(viii) *Insecurity and regression*. Tendency to flee change by seeking security in the past or in fantasy life. Example: reactionary appeals to 'fundamentalist' forms of traditional education.

>   (b) Guskin [23]: 'individual variables in knowledge
>   utilization'

(i) *Sense of competence and self-esteem*. Individuals with less confidence in their abilities are less willing to try out innovations. In their working lives, they would be more likely to reject the new and the strange because it constitutes a threat to their competence. Studies of teachers show a 'fear of failure' which make them more resistant to new practices than other professionals.

(ii) *Authoritarianism and dogmatism*. The authoritarian personality has a strong tendency to accept directives from dictatorial leaders and a rigid rejection of any changes emanating from outside sources. Such people are less open minded than others; they hold on for a longer time to an original interpretation about which they have felt certain. When faced with changes in their environment, they tend to respond slowly and only to see things that can be reconciled with their original reading of a situation. In clinical studies, teachers who scored low on the dogmatism scale were predisposed to accept educational innovations, while those scoring high accepted innovation only when proposed by dictatorial leaders.

(iii) *Feelings of threat and fear*. We have discussed this point. A person has a need for consistency in his self-image and tends therefore to distort new information in order to maintain that image.

(iv) *Self-fulfilling prophecies*. Our expectations of failure or success; effects of early experiences (when initial changes are exhausting, resistance increases); others' expectations of our failure or success.

47

(c) Harvey [21]: the 'conceptual systems approach'

Harvey holds that people have different 'cognitive styles'; they organize and present information in particular ways, closely related to their personality traits. Faced with a given situation, an individual will structure it and make sense out of it in ways compatible with his motives and subjective ends. People vary from highly concrete to highly abstract systems.

The highly concrete self-system has the following characteristics : tendency towards extreme, more polarized evaluations (good-bad, right-wrong, black-white); greater dependence on status and authority as guidelines to belief and action; intolerance of uncertainty, with a tendency to form judgements of novel situations more quickly; poorer capacity to act 'as if , to place himself in the position of another person, to visualize a hypothetical situation; holding of opinions with greater strength and greater certainty that opinions won't change with time; high conventionality and ethnocentrism; high score in dictatorialness (high need for structure, low flexibility, low encouragement of individual responsibility, high punitiveness, low diversity of activities).

Finally, let us look at two examples of resistance in action. Eichholz and Rogers [14] carried out an attitude survey of resistance to new educational media on the part of elementary school teachers. In their sample, eight types of 'rejection responses' appeared.

(i) *Rejection through ignorance*. When a given innovation was unknown, or its complexity led to misunderstanding: 'I don't always know what audio-visual materials are available'; I don't know how to use the movie projector'.

(ii) *Rejection through default*. 'I never use a tape recorder ... just don't use it, that's all'.

(iii) *Rejection by maintaining the status quo*. When the teacher did not accept an innovation because it had not been used in the past: 'I tend to do the teaching process mechanically, because the book does it that way'.

(iv)   *Rejection through social mores*. When the teacher believed
her colleagues did not find an innovation acceptable, and therefore did not use it herself: 'I don't use the museum. There
are only certain classrooms that visit the museum'.

(v)   *Rejection through interpersonal relationships*. By indi-
cating that friends did not use an innovation, or that a particular school environment made innovation unacceptable: 'The principal doesn't think less of a teacher for not using audio-visual
materials'.

(vi)   *Rejection through substitution*. 'I do more work with
charts and things like that than with audio-visual'.

(vii) *Rejection through fulfilment*. When the teacher was certain
of already knowing the 'best' or 'only' way to teach: 'I would
not take additional instruction in A-V materials because I think
you take those things you are interested in, and I am interested
in music and art'.

(viii) *Rejection through experience*. As in the recalling of an
incident when an innovation was tried and failed: 'The children
like filmstrips at the beginning because they are a novelty, but
after a while they get bored'.

   Eichholz and Rogers [14] also present a revised framework for
the identification of rejection responses. Fig. 8 tabulates typical responses they found for various forms of rejection, and diffe-
rentiates between 'real' and 'stated' reasons for rejection.

   The second example is a study of seven contested innovations
in the USA (including rural free delivery and women's suffrage).
The opponents were of four types : (a) those who favoured the
innovation but disagreed with the form it should take; (b) those
who created independent groups of their own to defeat the innovation; (c) those who were inspired or coerced into opposition by the
second group; (d) those whose resistance was only incidental or
situational, their real interests lying elsewhere.
   It is important to mention at this point that there is often
good cause for resistance. As all changes are not necessarily
warranted, resistance may be justified. The quality, value, relevance or feasibility of the proposals may be deficient at the
outset or at any point in implementation. This is most likely to
be so when the planners of change are alienated from the world of
those for whom they are planning. All too often in the case of

Fig. 8: A framework for the identification of forms of rejection

Form of rejection	Cause of rejection	State of subject	Anticipated rejection responses
1. Ignorance	Lack of dissemination	Uninformed	'The information is not easily available.'
2. Suspended judgment	Data not *logically* compelling	Doubtful	'I want to wait and see how good it is, before I try.'
3. Situational	Data not *materially* compelling	1. Comparing	'Other things are equally good.'
		2. Defensive	'The school regulations will not permit it.'
		3. Deprived	'It costs too much to use in time and/or money.'
4. Personal	Data not *psychologically* compelling	1. Anxious	'I don't know if I can operate equipment.'
		2. Guilty	'I know I should use them, but I don't have have time.'
		3. Alienated (or estranged)	'These gadgets will never replace a teacher.' ('If we use these gadgets, they might replace us.'
5. Experimental	Present or past trials	Convinced	'I tried them once and they aren't any good.'

innovations exported from one context to another, the technical assistance teams bringing in, say, an educational television network, a teacher training scheme or a new curriculum, neither perceive, understand nor value the basic purposes of the schools into which the innovation is to be imported. Their object is to make certain that the target audience accepts or 'buys' the innovation, with little concern for the durability or the depth of the adoption, not to mention the possibility that the innovation might be meaningless or harmful. A number of technological innovations have been so demanding of time, space and equipment that the servicing of the innovation has disrupted instructional practices elsewhere or has left other schools with fewer resources. In other cases, a new practice has set off a chain reaction of resentment among teachers, impatience among administrators and wariness among students and parents with the result that other sectors of the school have suffered even if the particular project was successful.

In general, when experts are unwilling to identify with or to be educated into the value system of those for whom their expertise is intended, they do a double disservice: they promote a new method or tool which is unlikely to survive — or, if it does survive, is unlikely to resemble the original method or tool proposed — and they leave the community or school with no greater capacity or internal resources to solve its own problems than were available before the experts came on the scene. The problem for local administrators or teachers is to differentiate between a change which poses a real threat and one which is resisted simply because it is new and feels alien.

2. THE INNOVATORS

Machiavelli wrote in *The Prince* that there was 'nothing more difficult to carry out nor more doubtful of success nor more dangerous to handle than to initiate a new order of things, for the reformer has enemies in all those who profit by the old order and only lukewarm defenders in all those who would profit by the new'. Who are those who stimulate, initiate, implement and institutionalize change in education?

Commenting on his compendium of case studies, Miles [37] describes innovative persons as strong, benevolent, high in intelligence and verbal ability, less bound by local group norms, more individualistic and creative, revealing authenticity and enthusiasm when persuading others, often rebellious, alienated, excessively

51

idealistic, emotionally stable, and prone to resentment and rebellion in the face of adversity or disillusionment.

A more clinical picture comes from Harvey [21] and his fourth 'conceptual system', characterized by a high degree of 'abstractness': a more complex, enriched mediational system with greater ability to depart from immediate situations ... less absolutism, greater relativism ... freedom to solve problems and evolve solutions without fear of punishment for deviating from established truth and social imperatives ... high task orientation, information seeking, exploratory behaviour, risk-taking, independence. On the Omnibus Personality Inventory, for example, such persons would score high on the autonomy (AU) and religious orientation (RO) scales. They may be described clinically as emancipated, liberal, non-authoritarian, generally open to new ideas and experiences, or as 'self-actualized'.

In an analysis of the innovative personality in developing countries [36], the higher innovator is described as someone who sees a coherent world about him which he feels will respond predictably to his efforts to change it; he trusts his own evaluation of his experience; he sees the surrounding world as applauding him if he achieves his goals; he has high needs for autonomy, achievement, order, help to others, and support from others. Similarly, Lazarsfield and Katz [27] characterize a person with a 'modern' orientation as follows: willingness to take risks, belief in scientific knowledge and in impersonal sources of information, sense of competence, faith in his capacity to control the environment. The opposing or 'traditionalist' personality places more trust in friends and family opinions than in scientific evidence and is prone to fatalism and conservatism.

Lippit [28] makes some interesting remarks on the personality characteristics of teachers. He found that teachers were more likely to be involved in the innovation diffusion process, if they: felt they had authority to direct their own classroom life, and were confident that they could do so effectively; were willing to share information about their classroom activities with their peers, with a minimum of fear of failure or rejection; were highly committed to the profession and willing to engage in discussion about professional matters.

As already mentioned, the key innovators in education are less the inventors than those who first adopt new ideas — the first 2.5 per cent at the beginning of the S-curve of adoption. Drawing on research on diffusion of innovations in rural sociology, industrial engineering and anthropology, Rogers [47] comes up with a useful 'world' picture of the innovator:

(i) *Innovators have relatively high social status*, in terms of education, prestige ratings and income.

(ii) *Innovators generally are young.* The young, Rogers argues, are less likely to be conditioned by traditional practices within the established culture. In a study of educational innovators, Lippitt [28] found them, however, to be younger and older than the mean. His guess was that older teachers who have returned to class-rooms after having raised their own children were willing to try out new ideas and practices, and that others were bored with doing the same thing year after year. The older teachers proved to be more potential adopters of innovations than the young, whereas the younger teachers were more potential innovators.

(iii) *Impersonal and cosmopolite sources of information are important to innovators.* When innovators decide to use a new idea, they cannot draw on the experience of others in their social system. As a result, innovators must secure new ideas from impersonal sources, such as the mass media, and from 'cosmopolite sources' outside their immediate environment. In studies of the diffusion of new drugs among physicians and of hybrid seed corn among farmers, the patterns were similar: early adopters attended more out-of-town meetings, read professional journals, made more frequent trips to the city and contacted several sources before making a judgement.

(iv) *Innovators are cosmopolite.* 'The cliques and formal organizations to which they belong are likely to include other innovators. They travel widely and participate in affairs beyond the limits of their system.' [47]. Teachers at more innovative schools usually acquire new educational ideas from outside their community.

(v) *Innovators exercise opinion leadership.*

(vi) *Innovators are likely to be viewed as deviants by their peers and by themselves.* Schon's definition of the 'product champion', the man who sponsors a new business or industrial product against all opposition, is a case in point. Schon [49] pictures him as 'a man of strong will, atttracted to risk, set against the esta-blished order, with great energy and the capacity to invite and withstand disapproval.'

The best-known typology of the deviant innovator is that of Barnett [102]. He classified the following: the 'dissident', who

53

has consistently refused to identify himself with some of the conventions of his group; the 'indifferent', who is prepared to accept new ideas because he has not committed himself to a custom or an ideal of society; the 'disaffected', who is at odds with society as a result of such variables as marginal status, disillusionment, frustration, generalized social anxiety, guilt depression, circumvention by specified enemies; and the 'resentful', who is susceptible to a suggestion of change because he has little and often nothing to lose by acceptance.

As a footnote to Barnett, Katz [27] claims that in traditional or underdeveloped communities, the most marginal and disaffected are the innovators, whereas in the most industrialized countries, the situation is reversed. This remark has obvious implications for the politics of educational innovation.

Deviant innovators are often people who are have been imperfectly socialized and therefore do not know what they are meant to do in a given situation. They may be more free to take initiative than those who have been more socially 'programmed'. Alternatively, they might be individuals living in a social system in which they realize that they cannot attain socially legitimate goals by the accepted means, and are driven as a result to use new and deviant means to reach their objectives.

V Traits and functions of innovative institutions

Society created such institutions as schools in order to attain
certain general goals and other more specific objectives which it
found could not easily be achieved without organization. The organizational forms in education are professional, collegial, and
bureaucratic, the object being to facilitate a series of interactions between teachers and students via formal instruction in the
classroom. We have seen that the more 'innovative' schools monitor
those interactions more closely and will attempt to modify them
the better to serve their instructional objectives. We now propose
to look more closely at the structural characteristics that distinguish these innovative systems from those which more often
resist or reject improvements.

Sociologists and industrial psychologists have written at
length about the characteristics of innovative organizations. A
typical description is that of Steiner's [51] 'creative' organization, which encourages 'idea men', has open channels of communication, is decentralized and diversified, encourages contact with
outside sources, employs heterogeneous types of personnel, uses an
objective and fact-finding approach and is willing to try out new
ideas on their merit, regardless of the status of their originator.
In short, a creative organization is a collection of creative persons who do not get in one another's way.

For Mort [41], schools with 'high adaptability' were those in
which teachers were more highly trained and more receptive to
modern educational ideas; where administrators provide active support for adaptations rather than remaining neutral; and where the
public's attitudes favoured modern practices. Mort tried to prove
that the key dependent variables were (a) higher financial support
and (b) higher level of parental education and occupation, but
research in other parts of the USA and in other countries has
not corroborated that thesis. Marcum's [24] study, using the Organizational Climate Description Questionnaire, showed that innovative schools had open climates (on a continuum of open-autonomous-

controlled-familiar-paternal-closed), higher expenditures, younger staff members, larger professional staffs, and staff members who remained in the system a shorter period of time.

We can group a good many of these characteristics around Miles' ten dimensions of 'organizational health' [38]. In general terms, a healthy organization 'not only survives its environment, but continues to cope adequately over the long haul, and continuously develops and extends its surviving and coping abilities.' However, in scanning Miles' list, we should point out that social psychologists have only begun in recent years to design instruments which can measure the presence or absence of these properties. On the following ten dimensions, many of which are drawn by analogy from the behaviour of persons or small groups, the first three are related to tasks, organizational goals, the transmission of messages and the way in which decisions are made; the second group (iv to vi) refers to the internal state of the organization; finally there are four dimensions which deal with growth and changefulness.

(i) *Clarity and acceptance of goals*. In a healthy organization, members are reasonably clear about goals and their acceptability. Goals must be achievable with available resources and be appropriate, i.e., more or less congruent with the demands of the environment. Elsewhere, Miles [39] calls for instruments and work methods in schools for specifying areas of vagueness and dissent about goals and for increasing understanding of goals through discussion. Instruments are needed to help teachers assess precisely what the short-run consequences of their work have been. We also need routine behavioural data (on morale, perceived norms, conflict) as much as we do information on budgets, scheduling and staffing.

(ii) *Adequacy of communication*. 'Since the organizations are not simultaneous face-to-face systems like small groups, the movement of information within them becomes crucial... This involves distortion-free communication vertically, horizontally and across the boundary of the system to and from the surrounding environment ... People have the information they need and have gotten it without exerting undue efforts.' [38]

As a corollary for education systems, we might add such indicators as adequacy of communication between teachers (since teacher isolation is probably a result of defensiveness), between teachers and administrators, between teachers and children. For the last item, the requirement is whether adults can hear, and use, what children have to say [39]. Similarly, the adequacy of communication between child socialization agencies, including parents, could be measured.

(iii) *Optimal power equalization*. Subordinates can influence upwards, and can perceive that their superiors can do the same with their superiors. Units stand in an inter-dependent relationship to one another, with less emphasis on the ability of one unit to control the entire operation.

(iv) *Resource utilization*. A healthy organization, like a healthy individual, works to its potential: people are neither overloaded nor idling; there is a close correspondence between their personal characteristics and the demands of the system. People have a sense of learning and developing while in the process of making their contribution to the organization.

(v) *Cohesiveness*. The organization knows 'who it is'. Its members feel attracted to membership. They want to stay with the organization, be influenced by and have an influence on it. Lippitt also stresses this point [28]. He asked teachers to comment on what characteristics hinder or facilitate innovation, with reference to the teaching practice itself, physical and temporal arrangements, peer and authority relations and personal attitudes. It appeared that teachers who felt that they had an influence on other teachers and on school policy were likely to share information, new ideas and their own problems with others. Those who felt alienated from colleagues saw no point in communicating since they were convinced that no one would listen.

(vi) *Morale*. The sense of well-being or satisfaction, as judged from individual sentiments or responses. Despite the vagueness of this concept, behavioural scientists have isolated some of the components of high and low morale. Carl Rogers [45] speaks often of 'psychological safety', a sort of 'trust', and of 'psychological freedom', or 'openness'. Schools with qualities of trust and openness — as measured by the interpersonal relations and norms perceived to exist in the system by school personnel — tend to create a psychological climate favouring change and innovation.

(vii) *Innovativeness*. 'A healthy system would tend to invent new procedures, move towards new goals, produce new kinds of products, diversify itself and become more rather than less differentiated over time. In a sense, such a system could be said to grow, develop and change, rather than remain routinized and standard.' [38].

57

In structural terms, there are a number of implications here. School systems with these properties could be expected to institutionalize innovation: to devote space, time and money for personal career and organizational development programmes; to set up change-generating and experimental units with a research and development function; to provide rewards for innovators; to install 'environmental scanning' mechanisms whereby new developments in neighbouring schools, in community agencies and in ministerial policy-making are applied to the school itself.

(viii) *Autonomy*. A healthy organization is independent from the environment in the sense that it does not respond passively to demands from without, nor destructively or rebelliously to perceived demands. Like the healthy individual in his transactions with others, the school system would not treat its responses to the community as determining its own behaviour.

(ix) *Adaptation*. The idea is that of being in realistic, effective contact with the organization's surroundings. Its ability to bring about corrective change should be faster than the change cycle in the community.

(x) *Problem-solving adequacy*. 'The issue is not the presence or absence of problems, but the manner in which the person, group or organization copes with problems ... [in] an effective system, problems are solved with minimal energy; they stay solved; and the problem-solving mechanisms used are not weakened, but maintained or strengthened' [38]. Conflicts are treated as an indicator that changes are needed.

By the way of a resumé, Miles' concept of organizational health can be respresented more dynamically in a schematic chart (Fig. 9).

Fig. 9: Model of organization functioning and change environment.

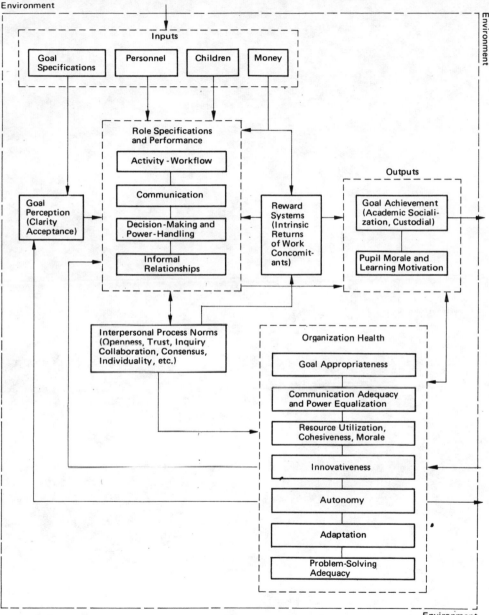

Fig. 9: Model of organization functioning and change environment

VI Planning and executing change

1. OVERVIEW OF MODELS

A very suspicious aspect of the literature on innovation is that
much of it analyses changes that have already taken place. The
studies are based on histories of more or less unplanned change
from which models are made of how in fact the process took place
and 'strategies' are drawn up to show how the process might have
been accelerated. We shall know a lot more about the dynamics of
change when we can control a given innovation from its genesis to
its full adoption, rather than re-create it after the fact.

Nonetheless, these case studies are justified in that one of
the objectives was to identify a natural process of change. By
tracing the sequence of events, we can isolate the phases of change
as they took place naturally, in order to take account of these
interactions when drawing up a planned sequence.

As we have seen, these phases differ according to the analyst.
the rural sociology model (awareness-interest-evaluation-trial-
adoption) foresees a different pattern and observes the process
from a different vantage point from the theory-into-practice model
or the problem-solving model. Each, in turn, as it views the change
process differently, implies a different strategy and a different
series of techniques in order to bring about the change more easily and more perfectly the next time round.

The literature contains three principal types of models illus-
trating how change takes place. Let us first take a quick look at
them, before examining them in detail. The first, *a theory-into-
practice* model or 'research and development' model, views the process as a rational sequence of phases, by which an innovation is
invented or discovered, developed, produced and disseminated to
the user. The innovation is not analysed from the viewpoint of the
user — who is presumably passive. Nor does research begin as a set
of answers to specific human problems, but rather as a set of facts
and theories which are then turned into ideas for useful products

61

and services in the development phase. The knowledge is then mass-produced and diffused to those for whom it might be useful [23].

This model is distinctly American in its emphasis on the translation of basic research into applied knowledge. 'It is assumed that medical progress is based on progress in the basic biological sciences and that engineering ... has been made possible by advances in the physical sciences. Usually there is only a dim understanding of how the knowledge gets transformed into something useful, but the firm belief remains that somehow it filters down.' [23]. Similarly, in Eastern European and Latin European systems, where research and development activities are centralized at the ministerial level and dissemination takes place only after a certain number of controlled experiments have been carried out, we have a variation on the theory-into-practice model. There is, however, an assumption that links exist between the research and practice worlds. Havelock [23] illustrates the 'interface' in diagrammatic form (Fig. 10).

The *social interaction* model emphasizes the aspect of diffusion, the movement of messages from person to person and system to system. Widely used in medicine and agriculture, it stresses the importance of inter-personal networks of information, of opinion leadership, personal contact and social integration. The idea is that each member in the system will proceed through the awareness-adoption cycle through a process of social communication with his colleagues. In a number of decentralized systems, notably the British , this strategy takes the form of convincing a respected administrator or teacher of the usefulness of a new device or practice, and then facilitating the process whereby colleagues come into contact with the new practitioner while he is using the innovation. The Swedish system, with its heavy investment in mass media and public information (80 million crowns annually), relies heavily on social interaction techniques.

The problem-solving model is built round the user of the innovation. It assumes that the user has a definite need and that the innovation satisfies that need. Thus the process is from problem to diagnosis of a need then to trial and adoption. Very often an external change-agent is required to counsel individuals on possible solutions and implementation strategies, but the emphasis is on client-centred collaboration rather than on manipulation from without. At first view, this participatory approach appears to be highly Scandinavian, although most of the problem-solving strategies have been designed in the United Kingdom and the USA. The

Fig. 10: The interface of research and practice.

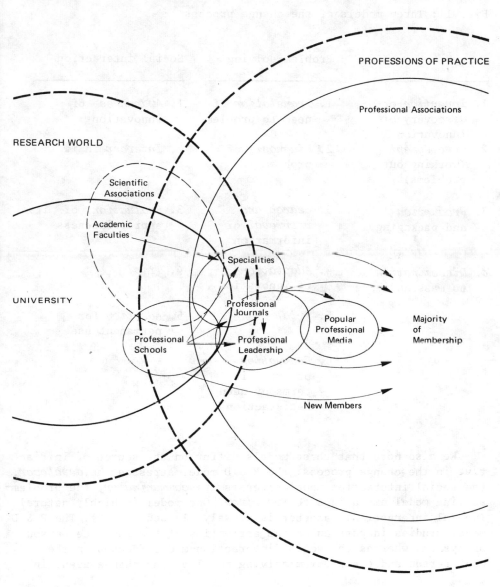

PROFESSIONS OF PRACTICE

Professional Associations

RESEARCH WORLD

Scientific
Associations

Academic
Faculties

Specialities

UNIVERSITY

Professional
Journals

Professional
Schools

Professional
Leadership

Popular
Professional
Media

Majority
of
Membership

New Members

way in which the process of change is conceived in the three
models is reconstituted in Fig. 11. [23]

Fig. 11: Three models of the change process

R & D	Problem-solving	Social interaction
1. *Invention* or discovery of innovation	1. *Translation* of need to problem	1. *Awareness* of innovation
2. *Development* (working out problems)	2. *Diagnosis* of problem	2. *Interest* in it
3. *Production* and packaging	3. *Search and retrieval* of information	3. *Evaluation* of its appropriateness
4. *Dissemination* to mass audience	4. *Adaptation* of innovation	4. *Trial*
	5. *Trial*	5. *Adoption* for permanent use
	6. *Evaluation* of trial in terms of need satisfaction	

We also note that these models differ on the source of initiative in the change process: the R & D model stresses the *developer*,
the social interaction model stresses the *communicator*, the problem-
solving model emphasizes the *receiver*. One model is highly natural
(social interaction): another is closely planned (R & D). The R & D
model studies in particular the activities of the resource person
or system, whereas the social interaction model focuses on the
user person and the problem-solving model on the change agent in

interaction with the user. Finally, Havelock [23]points out that the dissemination strategies in each model are different: one-way media for information and training (R & D); two-way involvement between sender and receiver (problem-solving); and a variety of transmission media (social interaction).

Fig. 12 enables the models and the sequence of events within each to be compared (see following page).

2. OVERVIEW OF STRATEGIES

Operationally, we mean by a strategy a set of policies underlying specific action steps (or tactics) expected to be useful in bringing about the lasting installation of a particular innovation [37]. This set of policies must take into account the innovation itself, the process of change, the characteristics of 'target' individuals or groups, and the nature of the system adopting the innovation.

There is, of course, no one strategy which can be applied to all types of innovations, processes, adopting groups and adopting systems. Experience has shown, however, that certain combinations or sequences are more effective than others and that certain preconditions must be met if any progress is to be made. For example, Watson [39] argues that structural approaches achieve the best results. Effective change sequences in schools usually involve structures first, altered interaction processes next and attitudes last. Watson claims that so long as the one-teacher-per-classroom model is maintained, it will be impossible to create the situation of interdependency and contact which leads to diffusion of new practices. As a result, such a structural change as the creation of team teaching units is seen to have brought about more changes in teacher sensitivities and skills than could have been achieved through human relations training with a staff operating within the self-contained classroom system.

Watson also thinks that all strategies should take as much account of resisting forces in the adopter as of tactics for bringing about adoption..He lists five pre-conditions for any successful attempt at institutional change: (i) participants must feel that the project is their own and not wholly devised by outsiders; (ii) the project must have the whole-hearted support of senior of officials of the system; (iii) the project must be in fairly close accord with the values and ideals of participants; (iv) the participants should experience support, trust, acceptance and confidence

Fig. 12: Stages typically included in models of change within three schools of research.

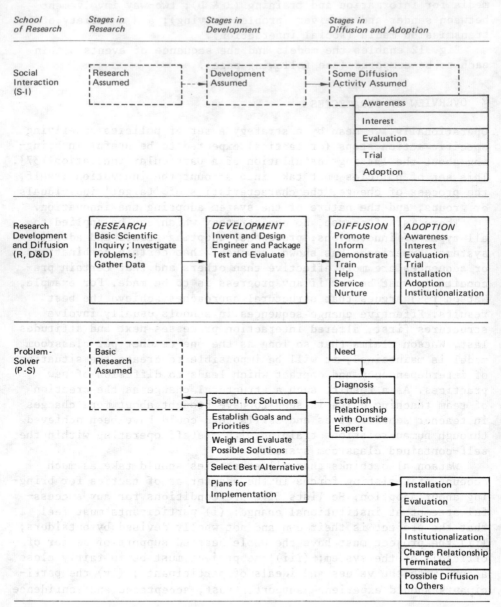

School of Research	Stages in Research	Stages in Development	Stages in Diffusion and Adoption	
Social Interaction (S-I)	Research Assumed	Development Assumed	Some Diffusion Activity Assumed	Awareness / Interest / Evaluation / Trial / Adoption
Research Development and Diffusion (R, D&D)	RESEARCH Basic Scientific Inquiry; Investigate Problems; Gather Data	DEVELOPMENT Invent and Design Engineer and Package Test and Evaluate	DIFFUSION Promote Inform Demonstrate Train Help Service Nurture	ADOPTION Awareness Interest Evaluation Trial Installation Adoption Institutionalization
Problem-Solver (P-S)	Basic Research Assumed	Need → Diagnosis → Establish Relationship with Outside Expert	Search for Solutions / Establish Goals and Priorities / Weigh and Evaluate Possible Solutions / Select Best Alternative / Plans for Implementation	Installation / Evaluation / Revision / Institutionalization / Change Relationship Terminated / Possible Diffusion to Others

in their relations with one another; (v) participants must feel
that their autonomy and security are not threatened.

The last is particularly important in projects aimed at teachers, who are likely to reject any proposal which they feel does
not suit their own style of classroom management.

The stategy adopted in a highly bureaucratic, centralized system is bound to be different from that used in a decentralized,
more professionalized framework. Similarly, the potential adopters
will be sensitive to different tactics in the two systems. Guba
[20] gives a topology of strategies which depend on the nature of the
adopter. More specifically, Guba's list is a collection of different types of motivation and intimidation: value strategy — the
adopter is viewed as a professional to whom an appeal can be made
in terms of value priorities (e.g., on behalf of 'what is best for
children'); rational strategy — the adopter can be convinced on the
basis of hard data and logical arguments of the utility, feasibility and effectiveness of the innovation; didactic strategy — the
adopter is willing, but untrained; psychological strategy — the
adopter has needs for acceptance, involvement and inclusion which
can be used to influence him; economic strategy — the adopter is
compensated for agreeing to adopt or is deprived of resources if
he refuses; authority strategy — the adopter can be compelled by
orders from hierarchical superiors.

Each of these strategies is then related to six diffusion
techniques: telling, showing, helping, involving, training and
intervening. What should be 'told' in relation to a rational strategy — scientific facts — would be different from what should be
'told' in relation to a psychological strategy — experiences. Decentralized systems must rely on the more indirect methods (rational,
psychological, value priority) while more centralized systems might
use the authority or economic strategies. Guba ends with the remin-
der that techniques should be consistent with the strategy they
employ: 'There is no point in quoting facts and figures if the
only effective way to approach an adopter is to buy him.'

Fig. 13 depicts the link between techniques of intervention
and the various phases of the change process [22].

Fig. 13: Co-ordinating change agent activities with adoption activities.

CHANGE AGENT ACTIVITIES

CLIENT ACTIVITIES

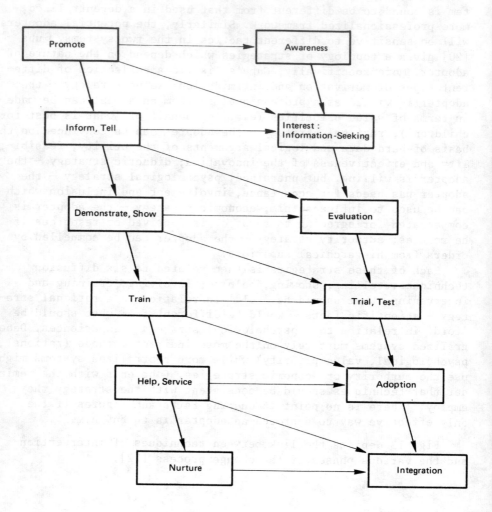

Chin and Benne [12] have regrouped these categories into basic types. The new clusters are useful not only because they correspond more closely to our three process models, but also because they can be referred more specifically to different kinds of ministerial or policy-making traditions.

(i) *Empirical-rational approach*. The implication here is that men are rational, and that they will follow their rational self-interest once it is shown them. The innovation will be adopted if it can be rationally justified and if it can be shown that the adopter will benefit by the change. The assumption is also that reason determines the process of initiating innovations; thus scientific investigation is the best way of extending knowledge, from basic research to practical application. Such a strategy has its best results when the public is ready to accept a new invention. When there are difficulties, a public information campaign is often used. The approach is least successful when there is strong resistance among potential adopters.

(ii) *Normative-reeducative approach*. The assumption here is that the adopter is not passive, waiting for solutions from without, but rather in active search for a solution to his problems. The strategy is based a psychotherapeutic model of change-agent (counsellor) and adopter (client) in which, with the collaboration of the agent, the client works out his changes for himself. The aim is less technical training than changing of attitudes and values, with two principal objectives: (a) to improve the problem-solving capacities of the client or adopting system, in particular the human relationships as these bear on the functioning of the system itself; (b) to bring self-clarity and personal development to the individuals within the system, on the premise that personal changes will lead eventually to organizational changes.

(iii) *Power-coercive approach*. The strategy here is to use political and economic sanctions to enforce change. This approach is necessary when legislation is involved (comprehensive schools, new examinations, better trained teachers, new curricula), but is also the common manner of bringing about less sweeping reforms in countries where the teaching and administrative staff are expressly hired as civil servants. We should bear in mind the fact that making an order does not mean that the decision can be carried out.

To be adopted at the personal level, most innovations require new knowledge, skills, attitudes, often new value orientations. At the social level, there must be changes in norms, roles, and relationships.

3. THREE MODELS OF HOW CHANGE TAKES PLACE.

Research, development and diffusion model

The majority of models and strategies in education are based on the transfer from theory to practice. The process of change is seen as an orderly sequence, beginning with the identification of a problem or the generation of an idea, proceeding through development (of solutions or prototypes) and ending with the diffusion of the product to a target group. The major emphasis is on the planning of change on a large scale, for which specialized institutions (national research agencies, laboratories, experimental units) are required for scientific research, development and rigorous testing and evaluation. Mechanisms must also be included for distributing the innovation and installing it in a target system. The prototypes of this model are to be found in industry, defence and, in several countries, in agriculture.

Havelock [23] lists the major characteristics in this model in the following way. First the model assumes that innovation is a rational sequence of activities which moves from research to development to packaging before dissemination takes place. Secondly, the model implies planning on a massive scale, completed by a division of labour, the subdivision of knowledge flow into different functional elements which link the research community and product organizations to practitioners and consumers. Third, there must be a clearly defined target audience, a specified passive consumer who will accept the innovation if it is delivered on the right channel, in the right way and at the right time. This is to be assured by a process of scientific evaluation at every stage of development and dissemination. Finally, this model accepts high initial development costs before any dissemination activity, because it foresees a gain in the long run in terms of efficiency quality and capacity to reach a mass audience.

Each of the four steps involved in the model — research, development, diffusion and aoption — is itself divided into sub-tasks with specific objectives, criteria and relationship to the overall process of change. The most complex and complete prototype is that of Guba and Clark [19] which is shown in Fig. 14 in a highly condensed form.

In no country, admittedly, do mechanisms exist which perform any one of these tasks as comprehensively as outlined by Guba and Clark, not to mention the lack of a sophisticated co-ordinating agency. In most countries, research activities are performed in universities by individuals carrying out individual rather than common projects. Team research — required for major research and development activities — is unknown in education and only a recent phenomenon in industry. Most activities are theoretical, unidisciplinary, poorly funded and suffering from a shortage of trained personnel. As to development, Guba [20] himself points out that neither practitioners nor researchers are particularly competent to undertake it and that each assumes that the other has the responsibility of inventing and designing prototypes. This phase is also particularly expensive. Until recently, it has been left to commercial interests (publishers and manufacturers), who hired the subject-matter specialists and technologists required for preparing, engineering and packaging new materials. Such agencies as the American regional laboratories and British Nuffield projects are embryonic attempts to install a development capacity within the educational network itself.

Finally, the model itself underestimates the stages of diffusion and adoption by assuming that the enlightened self-interest of the practitioner will lead to eventual incorporation of the innovation. There is also the fact that in almost all countries there exist in fact no agencies aside from commercial salesmen and verbal recommendation for the dissemination of new practices. In his study of the American physics curriculum reform (PSSC), Marsh [32] noted the slow rate of adoption owing to the 'materials centred approach' of the developers, who had no deliberate plan for delivering the materials to teachers. On the other hand, the science and maths programmes developed by the National Science Foundation were well disseminated because (a) they were designed as complete units; (b) instructional materials were available; (c) in-service training was offered to the teacher at no cost; (d) the materials could be used by one teacher without disturbing the work of others [6]. The key factor here is clearly the amount of help available to the teacher at the outset.

Fig. 14 : A classification schema of change process

	Research	Development		Diffusion
		Invention	*Design*	*Dissemination*
Objective	To advance knowledge	To formulate a new solution to an operating problem or to a class of operating problems, i.e. *to innovate*	To order and to systematize the components of the invented solution; to construct an innovation package for institutional use, i.e., *to engineer*	To create widespread awareness of the invention among practitioners i.e., *to inform*
Criteria	Validity (internal and external)	Face Validity (appropriateness) - - - Estimated Viability - - - Impact (relative contribution)	Institutional Feasibility - - - Generalizability - - - Performance	Intelligibility - - - Fidelity - - - Pervasiveness - - - Impact (extent to which it affects key targets)
Relation to Change	Provides basis for invention	Produces the invention	Engineers and packages the invention	Informs about the invention

| | Adoption | | |
Demonstration	Trial	Installation	Institutionalization
To afford an opportunity to examine and assess operating qualities of the invention, i.e., *to build conviction*	To build familiarity with the invention and provide a basis for assessing the quality, value, fit, and utility of the invention in a particular institution, i.e., *to test*	To fit the characteristics of the invention to the characteristics of the adopting institution, i.e., *to operationalize*	To assimilate the invention as an integral and accepted component of the system, i.e., *to establish*
Credibility - - Convenience - - Evidential Assessment	Adaptability - - - Feasibility - - - Action	Effectiveness - - - Efficiency	Continuity - - - Valuation - - - Support
Builds conviction about the invention	Tries out the invention in the context of a particular situation	Operationalizes the invention for use in a specific institution	Establishes the invention as a part of an ongoing program; converts it to a "non-innovation"

Often, of course, this help comes from outside the school
system itself, in the form of a consultant or 'facilitator' who
can adapt the device to individual practices. Jung [25] talks of
the 'trainer' who can provide horizontal linking (ways of communicating with and learning from other teachers or others concerned
with child socialization in the community) or vertical linking
(access to new materials or to the new techniques of behavioural
science which can be useful at the classroom level — sociometric
tests, counselling, group dynamics, role playing).

Brickell [6] argues that there are three separate processes
— which he calls 'design, evaluation and dissemination' — which
are distinct and irreconcilable. He claims that it is one thing
to design a new way of teaching, another to find out whether the
invention is any good, and still another to demonstrate it for the
purpose of persuading others to adopt it. The circumstances which
are right for one process are wrong for the others. The design
phase flourishes in 'enriched and free' circumstances (a task
force, an isolated setting). Conditions seldom permit a group of
talented men to be paid and allowed to concentrate specifically
on an invention. The evaluation phase, on the other hand, requires
a controlled, closely observed, 'unfree' environment in order to
determine what the innovation will accomplish under specific conditions. Finally, the ideal conditions for dissemination by demonstration are ordinary, unenriched and normal — everyday situations.

Brickell points out that medicine, agriculture and industry
have created agencies for each of these functions, whereas education either has never viewed the process as a whole or has invested
all three irreconcilable functions in one institution, as in a
university experimental school 'laboratory'. He proposes the following network: a centralized research agency for administration of
new projects, teams of temporary programme design 'task forces',
temporary evaluation groups from local universities and, for the
dissemination phase, regional development units serving 10-20
school systems and providing demonstration facilities and teacher
training, with continued monitoring after the innovation is
installed.

One of the most sophisticated examples of the research and
development model is that of Research for Better Schools (RBS);
an agency responsible for the implementation and field testing of
an individually paced mathematics programme (IPI) at the primary
school level. The basic research and development of prototypes for

74

evaluation is carried out by the University of Pittsburgh in its
Learning Research and Development Centre, while the materials are
mass-produced by a commercial publishing firm. After the materials
are developed (the research-invention-design cycle of Guba and
Clark) at the university, RBS enters into a mutual agreement with
a number of school districts for preliminary diffusion (the dissem-
ination-demonstration-trial phase of the model). Staff training
is provided for; 'monitoring engineers' are sent into the adopting
districts to supervise in-service training and demonstration activities; the preliminary evaluation is made. The adoption phase
(installation-institutionalization) contains a process of 'controlled participation' as the teachers experiment with the new materials. It also includes further training of administrators and
supporting staff and continued monitoring of the new programme at
work through monthly visists over a fixed period of time. When the
laboratory phase is over, widespread dissemination is sought through
a similar sequence, aided by the mass production of the instructional materials.

Social interaction model.

In this process, the unit of analysis is the individual receiver,
with the focus on the receiver's perception of and response to knowledge coming from without. As studies in this area have shown that
the most effective means of spreading information about an innovation is by means of personal contact, the key to adoption is the
social interaction among members of the adopting group [23]. Researchers usually concentrate on an innovation that appears in a
concrete diffusable form (fertilizer, new drug, audio-visual aids,
new curriculum or textbook) and trace its flow through the social
system of the adopters. They study in particular the effects of
social structure and social relationships on the fate of innovations.

Research has shown fairly conclusively that all individuals go
through the same adoption sequence. We have sketched this process
in Chapter III (Fig. 7) and may now elaborate further:

(i) *Awareness*. The individual is exposed to the innovation but
lacks complete information about it, or may not be motivated to
seek further information. He is generally passive, in that awareness does not come about as the result of a need, but rather
creates a need for the innovation.

(ii) *Interest*. The individual seeks information about the innovation, but has not yet judged its utility in terms of his own
situation.

(iii) *Evaluation*. This is the period of 'mental trial', when the
individual applies the innovation to his present and anticipated
situation, and then decides whether or not to try it. In education,
what is essential here is whether or not the teacher is authorized
to try out a new device or practice — seldom the case in highly
centralized systems.

(iv) *Trial*. If the mental trial is favourable, he uses the innovation on a small scale, in order to judge its utility in his own
situation.

(v) *Adoption*. The results of the trial are considered, after
which the decision is made to adopt or reject the innovation.

At each stage, the potential adopter generally turns to different sources of information. These sources can be personal or impersonal, the latter referring to various types of media (print and
non-print). Media tend to play a major role during the 'awareness'
and 'interest' stages, whereas personal sources predominate in the
final three stages. In a number of rural sociology and medical studies, it was reported that media and commercial sources brought the
first news of an innovation, but that colleagues, friends and professional sources were required to legitimate decisions about adopting or rejecting.
These studies also revealed that early adopters or 'influen-
tials' greatly influence later adopters. The early adopters may be
the 'cosmopolites' mentioned earlier, who have read more, travelled
more widely, had more contact with experts and are more highly
educated; senior administrators who can enforce compliance through
formal leadership; so-called 'opinion leaders' to whom others turn
for advice; 'gatekeepers', who are the informal leaders in a system
(head of teachers' union, head of clique of senior teachers, com-
mittee chairman, inspector) and who can aid or hinder the adoption
of a new idea or practice. A strategy to introduce a given change
to members of a social system may be visualized as in Fig. 15 [22].

Fig. 15: A 'stepping stone' strategy for gaining group acceptance

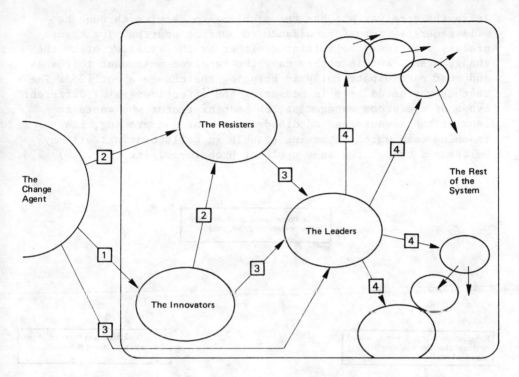

The key feature in all cases is the relation of leader to group. Psychologists have shown that identification in a group or with a leader plays an important role in diffusing new ideas since people will adopt and maintain attitudes and behaviours which they associate with their 'reference' group. Innovators are likely to be found in a greater variety and number of such reference groups and, as cosmopolites, are able to see personal relevance in ideas and things which their neighbours would perceive as alien. A society with large numbers of individuals who maintain diverse and overlapping reference group identifications will tend to be innovative [23].

Problem-solving model

It is the receiver who has the problems to resolve through he
will generally turn for guidance to outside sources. The change
process itself may be initiated either by the receiver or by the
change agent, but in either case the receiver must want to change
and must participate fully in bringing the change about [23]. The
teacher who needs help in measuring the effectiveness of different
types of classroom management, the administrator who wants to
look at the advantages and disadvantages of non-grading, the
teaching team which is having trouble in collaborating: all may
be assumed trough the same cycle of probelm-solving (Fig. 16) [22].

Fig. 16.

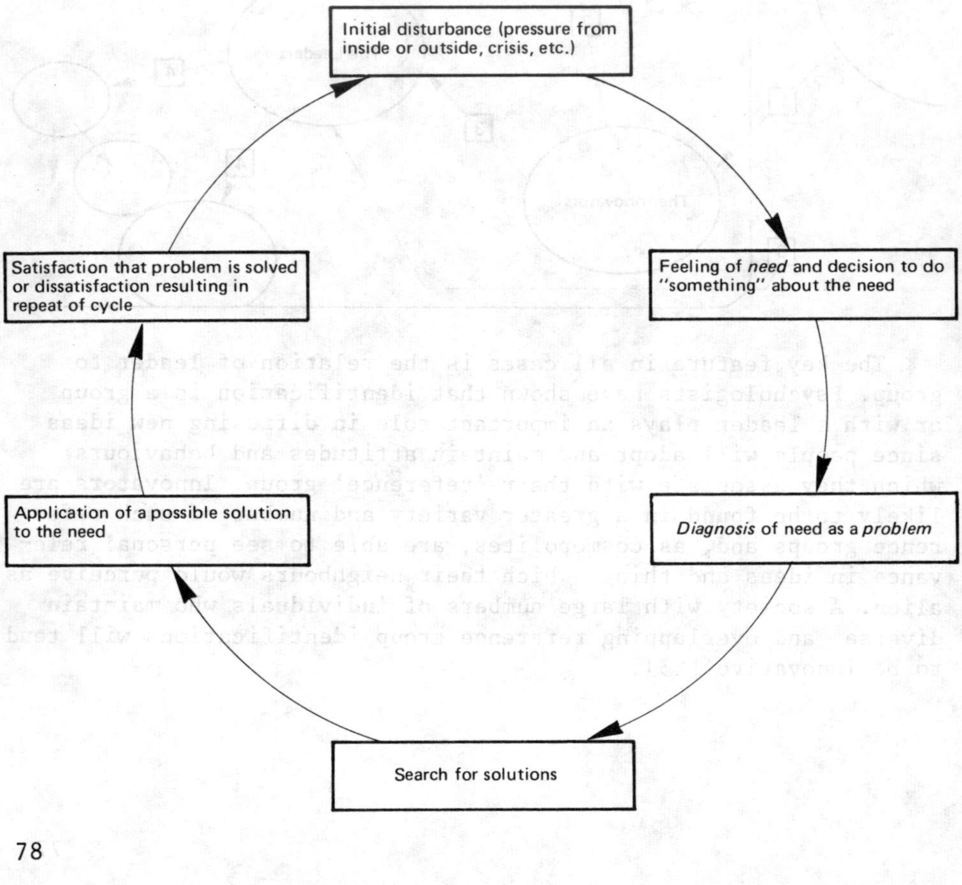

Initial disturbance (pressure from inside or outside, crisis, etc.)

Satisfaction that problem is solved or dissatisfaction resulting in repeat of cycle

Feeling of *need* and decision to do "something" about the need

Application of a possible solution to the need

Diagnosis of need as a *problem*

Search for solutions

If the school turns to an external consultant, the field of our diagram must be enlarged as in Fig. 17 [23].

Fig. 17: The problem-solver perspective

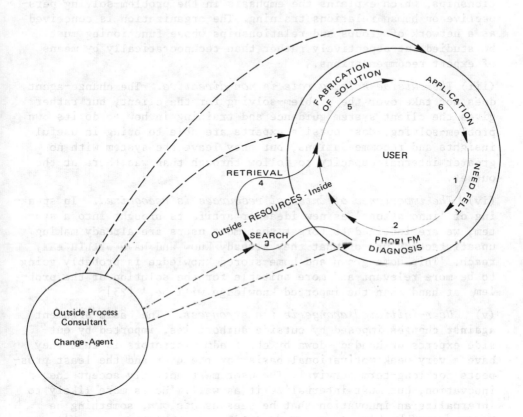

We can synthesize the basic properties of this approach into five points [23].

(i)   *The user is the starting place.* It is important to recognize that the interaction model is both inconclusive and potentially irresponsible. First, the process ends when the target audience accepts or 'buys' the innovation, without looking into the durability or depth of the adoption. Secondly, the social-interaction model is manipulative; there is little concern for the adopter's real needs or circumstances, nor for the fact that the innovation might be meaningless or harmful to him.

79

(ii) *Diagnosis comes before solutions are identified.* The model is highly clinical in the sense that more deeply seated problems are sought beneath the manifest symptoms. Most problems are concerned with difficulties of communicating and interpersonal relationships, which explains the emphasis in the problem-solving perspective on human relations training. The organization is conceived as a network of groups and relationships whose functioning must be studied introspectively rather than technocratically by means of expert recommendations.

(iii) *The outside helping role is non-directive.* The change-agent does not take over the problem-solving for the client, but rather gives the client system guidance and training in how to do its own problem-solving. Most outside experts are able to bring in useful insights and recommendations, but they leave the system with no greater internal capacity to follow through than was there at the outset.

(iv) *The importance of internal resources is recognized.* In speaking of 'innovations' as new ideas or artifacts brought into a system, we are inclined to forget that most users are already making unsatisfactory use of what they already know and have within easy reach. 'This home-grown and home-stored knowledge is probably going to be more relevant and more suitable for the solution of the problem at hand than the imported knowledge will be.' [23]

(v) *User-initiated change is the strongest.* The basic argument against changes imposed by outside authorities, imported by outside experts or handed down by chief administrators is that they have a very weak motivational basis for the user and the least prospects for long-term survival. The user must not only accept the innovation, but must internalize it as well. 'He is more likely to internalize an innovation that he sees as *his own*, something he has accepted by his own free and deliberate choice to meet his own specific need, and something that he has worked on himself to *adapt* to his own specific need.' [23]

The thesis of internal motivation is often used in the literature on change to legitimize participation, the active involvement of individuals who are affected by decisions in the decision-making process. The literature on social change has shown that people will accept innovations more readily if they understand them, perceive them as relevant and have helped to plan them. Often the process is accelerated by using group cohesiveness as a catalyst.

80

The fact that a group makes a decision or a commitment seems to cement the consensus more strongly in each member, while at the same time the interaction among members improves communications or leads to greater interdependence in the system at large. One American study [23] reported that teachers' participation in the policy-making process of the school led to less alienation, greater sharing of ideas, possibly better teaching and possibly greater receptivity to change. Research in other social science fields also indicates that members who are socially integrated into peer group structures — without being driven to conformism — are more innovative, i.e., more receptive to new ideas. As a footnote, most of the literature involving teachers suggests that the innovators operate neither alone nor in large groups, but in groups of two or three, generally in pairs having similar background and status.

The techniques used by change agents within the user system vary from large-scale operations (conference, games, *ad hoc* task forces, personnel assessment programmes, demonstrations) to more intensive group dynamics work akin to psychotherapy and counselling. As mentioned before, the objective is ordinarily twofold: to reeducate or 'unlearn' the individual, and group attitudes which brought on the problems in the first place, and to 'educate' or add new knowledge, skills, attitudes, practices. In most of the procedures used, participants are put into free environments, often in reclusion, where they can experiment with new roles or relationships in risk-free, controllable conditions. In these circumstances, participants tend to be more open and direct with one another; they will discuss common problems in such a way as to release long maintained misunderstandings, condemnation, prejudice or false information. Status and rank are minimized. Members begin to relate with less suspicion to one another and to the group. The basic principle is that increasing communication in free surroundings will lead people to see one another more objectively and to co-operate more readily. We must point out once again, however, that in few countries are such techniques in use or even conceivable, in view of the patterns of social interaction accepted between colleagues or between members of different levels of an administrative hierarchy. Among the various interaction techniques appropriate to education, three may be singled out [38].

(i) *Team training.* The members of a normal work group (for exam
ple, the school director and his master teachers) meet for several
days, away from their offices and classrooms, with consultant help.
They examine their own effectiveness as a problem-solving team, the
role of each member in the group and how it affects the group and
the person himself, and the operations of the group in relation
to its organizational environment. Under these circumstances, the
members usually improve their abilities to express feelings directly and to listen to — and understand — one another. Communications
and the successful management of internal conflicts generally
benefit.

(ii) *Survey feedback.* Data bearing on attitudes, opinions and
beliefs of members of the system are collected through question-
naires. Each group then examines its own summarized data in comparison with those for the organization as a whole. The exercise
of looking objectively at data referring to personal attitudes helps
to reduce feelings of being isolated or misunderstood; it also puts
problems in a framework where they can be dealt with, rather than
retaining them for blaming or scape-goating others or oneself. This
approach is being used increasingly in improving teacher-adminis-
trator relations.

(iii) *Organizational diagnosis and problem-solving.* Here, the
entire adult personnel of a school meets for several days to
identify problems, discuss the reasons for their existence, decide
on needed changes and to plan implementation of these changes
through regular channels and newly constructed ones. These new tar-
gets are then reviewed periodically. The objective is to strengthen
communications, group cohesiveness and problem-solving activity.
In a variation on this model, the members actually carry out a
controlled experiment, complete with before and after testing and
the use of control groups. Such a project includes a feedback
stage, in which the results are examined carefully and implications
are drawn for the functioning of the school.

   Miles [36] has observed that many of these techniques set off
an 'attitude cycle' among the participants. At first, members are
defensive and formal with one another. Each person withdraws, and
is reluctant to enter the system as a full participant until he
can be certain of his psychological safety. Next, an atmosphere
of play sets in. As role-playing and other types of self-awareness
techniques are being used, the individual comes to trust others

and anticipates rejection from them less; he becomes at the same time less self-critical and enters into the spirit of the undertaking. Then, members move in the direction of more interpersonal linking, acceptance and intimacy. This shades into a shared sentiment of group identity or *esprit de corps*, as the members are convinced that their relationships and responsibilities are meaningful. Finally, there is a sentiment of involvement or engagement in the goals of the system. The norms of the group are internalized in the individual members; such norms, for example, as equalitarianism, authenticity (openness and trust between members), inquiry, 'innovativeness' (favouring novelty and innovation), 'effortfulness' (a higher output of work, energy, effort). In short, the personal changes reinforce both relationship changes and the sentiment of group protection which is so important during the process of installing the innovation.

Perhaps the most ambitious undertaking which uses the problem-solving approach is the American COPED (Cooperative Project for Educational Development), which links behavioural scientists from a number of urban universities with some 25 school systems throughout the country. These change-agent teams hold seminars, lead task forces and collaborate with schools in implementing innovations and improving the skills of problem-solving among staff. At the same time, assessment instruments and successful strategies are devised in order better to monitor and accelerate the process of planned change in each of the participating schools.

In all such operations, however, there is a suggestion of social engineering, i.e., the assumption that an external group decides in advance on the type and manner of reform needed inside the education system and proceeds to install the innovation by means of sophisticated manipulation of the potential adopters. The target environment is analysed in terms of the probable responses to the proposed innovation, and a number of suitable rewards and reinforcement patterns are planned to ensure success. Although all such behavioural designs assume that the staff must understand the innovation, its requirements and its relation to the objectives of the school, the actual 'strategy' shows clearly that the school personnel are regarded as passive rather than active instruments in their own restructuring. The steps of such a strategy, as defined by Rubin [48] are: (i) analysis of the innovation's requirements in training, materials and linkage to existing system; (ii) initiation of motivating pressures through inducing dissatisfaction and illuminating the rewards; (iii) initiation of the influence strategy;

(iv) initiation of preparatory activities; (v) installing the innovation, etc.

4. THE CHOICE OF MODELS OR STRATEGIES

Separately, each of these models illuminates one perspective of the innovative process and suggests techniques for accelerating changes. The research and development model concentrates on the origins of the innovation, the problem-solving model on the dynamics of individual adoption and the social interaction model on wide diffusion throughout an organization or an educational system. The R & D model shows us that we lack institutional structures for designing and developing new ideas and materials; the problem-solving model shows the lack of processes for implementing changes once they are undertaken; the social interaction model shows that we have few vehicles for dissemination of an innovation to a larger public. To date, none of the models is fully developed in practice; nor has any attempt been made to combine the three approaches into a general paradigm.

As one would expect, different national systems have different ways of organizing the innovation process. Some operate by means of centralized research and diffusion bureaux (Poland, Norway, France); others rely on semi-autonomous research agencies (United Kingdom, USA). Some try to design all materials locally; other countries work on adapting new equipment or practices from abroad to local conditions. We can postulate that the three operations — research and development, vehicles for introducing change within a single institution and mechanisms for spreading innovations throughout the system — should be provided for in any strategy of change, but that the particular techniques and the sequence of adoption will vary from country to country. The important factor seems to be the creation of mechanisms over and above those needed to operate the education system — putting new agents in the environment, which will accelerate and supervise the different phases of the process.

VII Evaluating innovations

Until very recently, school systems have been neither equipped nor motivated to evaluate the outcomes of their teaching and learning activities. There is a tendency to assume that an innovation is good because it is new and if (a) it lasts, (b) it doesn't seem to be doing a poorer job than the practice which it replaced and (c) it doesn't disturb other activities in the school.

These are, in fact, some of the most important criteria to be applied when we are appraising changes in education. They may not, however, be directly related to the quality, value or relevance of the innovation for increasing learning, which is presumably the reason for which the innovation was introduced. School personnel are more preoccupied, it seems, with the feasibility of an innovation, in terms of probability of acceptance or potential disruption of current work, than with its potential for improving instruction. The principle reason for this, as we have shown, is that the proposal involves new ways of acting and interacting, often on the classroom level, which most school personnel are slow to accept. Often, therefore, the project becomes a personal conflict between those who want to change others and the others who do not want to be changed, who resent initiatives from above and outside purporting to improve *their* manner of doing *their* work. Since, in education systems, the effectiveness of new or old practices are hard to judge precisely, the quality or the stated objectives of the innovation soon become less important than its implantation. At the same time, the creators or champions of the change are convinced that the new practice is better than the existing one and tend to assume that systematic evaluation is not needed.

The most precise manner of evaluating an innovation is by trying it out on an experimental basis and comparing the results with those of a control group which is not using it. Experimental evaluation, however, is time-consuming and expensive and requires outside aid in design measurement and in assuring objectivity. Most schools systems are not willing to make the investment, which is often two or three times the cost of introducing the innovation itself. Nor can they afford the luxury of controlled situations and measurable procedures for a long period of time where school children are concerned. Finally, they are often unwilling to risk failure in the eyes of external evaluators, who tend to come from the university or the ministry itself. Unless these problems are ironed out in advance and unless evaluation funds are provided in the original plan, the system will use more intuitive methods for judging whether it should accept the change proposed or whether the innovation has been successful.

The second type of difficulty with experimental evaluation is the 'Hawthorne' or 'placebo' effect: the fact that the conditions surrounding an experiment tend to distort the results. All involved in the experiment will be aware that they are getting special attention or will be working harder to make the trial a success. Children and teachers will perform better, administrators will pay closer attention to the project, better classroom arrangements will be provided. Probably the best time to assess an innovation is when it is no longer an innovation, when the project can no longer call forth special energies, resources and enthusiasm [54].

Unless the objectives of the project are clearly defined, it may be impossible to measure the effectiveness of the innovation. We must know what the pupil is able to do, feel or think which he was not able to do, feel or think before the change or which he formerly did less well. We must also be able to isolate or specify the part played by a new device as distinct from the influence of the teacher or classroom or the child's emotional condition. And, of course, different indicators of effectiveness are required in, say, a team teaching project than in a new science curriculum.

The difficulty in measuring the role of an innovation in improving the learning of students is that not all such improvements — or not at any rate the most important ones — show up right away. The effects of new media, student group work, new study methods, revised teacher-training programmes, even new curricula, are usually delayed for a number of years. It is often argued that, since there are so many difficulties in measuring if and how a student is learning better or a teacher performing more effectively, we should concentrate on 'small aims' — slight but precise improvements in the speed or accuracy with which students spell, read or compute. The problem here is that the type of innovations which best pass this test in the short run are usually minor modifications of existing practices. As a result, the tendency is to concentrate on making the traditional system work better, rather than trying out major changes which could easily show poor results during the first few months or years but are likely to have a significant impact in the long run. It is often argued, in any event, that if educational innovations are clearly radical, they will have objectives which conventional evaluative instruments are incapable of measuring.

Here again, the basic question is one of goals. In an interesting international debate on the management of innovation [11], one participant claimed that there was no correlation between the innovativeness of an educational system and the level of achievement of its students. Both the United States and Sweden, with highly innovative systems, still ranked well below the leaders in international comparisons of mathematics achievement. The Scandinavian participant replied that factual knowledge and mathematics skills were less important in the Swedish system than were student developmental goals (less conformity, more critical awareness, greater adaptiveness, and creativity), and that innovations were directed to these objectives in particular. The secretariat found it difficult to frame a list of objectives which would all be considered as acceptable, sufficiently precise or even innovative in character.

In practical terms, the most frequent measurement is not the quality of the innovation but its durability. If the proposed project is rejected or discontinued, the innovation can be said to have failed. We have already outlined a number of possible reasons: incongruence with receivers' current practices and values, inadequate planning, insufficient training for adopters, lack of commitment, lack of resources, deficiencies in the innovation itself, lack of follow-up mechanisms, replacement by a superior innovation. There also appear to be a number of cases where a change is rejected or discontinued for a while and then adopted or readopted later.

In assessing the outcome of an innovation in terms of the original objectives set for it, we should take account of the authenticity of the innovation — whether the project has in fact been amended or otherwise modified. It can be determined fairly soon whether all the components of the innovation have actually been added to the system and whether the new practice is in use in the classroom. Brickell [7] distinguishes between 'components' (structural changes) and 'processes' (activities intended to follow from the structural changes). When the chief components are people, and is the case in instructional systems, the hoped-for process may not occur: the team teachers may not team teach; the television sets may not be turned on; the programmed text may not be assigned to the entire class a page at a time [7]. The recent national report on educational technology in the United States revealed that, although instructional films have been in schools for over 30 years, the average use of these films is lower than five films per teacher per year.

The basic question to be asked is whether the system has changed the innovation and if so in what way. Is the new curriculum in practice the same as in design? Is the subject content that is transmitted in class contained in the materials and called for in student tests similar to the original? 'Are the actual classroom operations which teachers employ from day to day ... [similar to] those in other schools where the innovation is being used sucessfully?... Do the local variations actually represent an intelligent tailoring of the innovation to fit local needs, as by adjusting the pace to match the abilities of local children? Or do they represent ... misunderstanding of the original, or incomplete adoption' [7]

Another series of indicators relates to the changes wrought by the innovation on the surrounding school system. Are the demands of time, space and equipment so great that the servicing of the innovation disrupts instuctional practices elsewhere or deprives them of resources? Does the new practice involve new rules (access to facilities, new grading methods, new staffing arrangements) which have not been changed in the school at large? Are teachers clear about the nature and objectives of the innovation? Are they protected from the risk of failure? Do they emotionally favour to the project? Is the administration firmly behind it and prepared to defend it before community and ministry officials?

It may be that, in the absence of scientific evidence as to whether the innovation results in increased learning, the most important criteria for evaluatin change are those related to the effect on the school's potential for change in the future. Paradoxically, the side effects of an innovation may count more than the direct effects. We get the flavour of this type of indicator from Miles' list of 'innovative success criteria' [37]:

(i) use of the innovation to accomplish broader purposes than originally envisaged;

(ii) existence of publications designed to draw the attention of a wider audience to the innovation;

(iii) improved attitudes or skills of the innovating group members which may affect their later innovativeness;

(iv) spread or diffusion of the innovation to other systems;

(v) stimulation of innovation in similar areas of school practices;

(vi) promotion or advancement of practitioners who have backed the innovation.

Finally, school systems can be evaluated in terms of the traits and functions which characterize innovative institutions, examined in Chapter V. The assumption would be that school systems with goal focus, adequacy of communication, power equalization, cohesiveness etc. would make more frequent and more effective changes — that they would set up experimental units, conduct research, invest in personnel development programmes, keep in contact with professional and community agencies. Similarly, such systems would presumably have a greater number of innovative people, those characterized by what Harvey called a high degree of 'abstractness' and clinically described as emancipated, liberal, non-authoritarian, open to new ideas, experienced and self-actualised.

VIII Summary and conclusions

Although education as a social system has been undergoing constant change, we have only recently begun to study the anatomy of the process in a systematic way. Few of these changes seem to have been planned in enough detail to predict or control the consequences of a new piece of legislation or a new method of reading. In general, we have tried to reconstruct the process after the event in order to make fewer errors on the next occasion. Only when the need for major reform in education has been recognized we can look more closely at the elements which aid or hinder the enactment of change and plan the process in such a way that the changes made are durable, measurable and similar to the original version of the innovation.

To conceive of change in education as a sort of social technology is, however, impractical in present conditions. Even in periods of accelerated social change, schools change very slowly and often require a great deal of pressure from outside to modify existing practices. Society has, in fact, created such institutions as schools in order to ensure social continuity, and has hired professionals to work in them. These professionals tend to resist novelty more subbornly and initiate new methods or practices less frequently than professionals in other sectors. Reforms are also inhibited by the absence of persons with the role of 'change agent' and of information about new possibilities. School goals are multiple and often contradictory. Schools have few resources for trying out new methods and provide no rewards for staff who innovate. It is difficult to prove that one teaching or learning method is better than another or to publicize malpractices; hence there is little impetus to reform.

Educational innovation is a complex subject because it must be studied at several levels: at the level of the individuals being changed or changing others, at the institutional level, at the community level and in the wider environment in which some innovations are acceptable while others conflict with existing values.

Innovations are rarely installed on their merits. The main factor appears to be the relative importance attached to the anticipated advantages and threats of the change in the eyes of the persons affected. In education, change seldom involves physical objects but rather persons, who are called upon to alter their way of looking at things and their habits of dealing with children and with other adults. Such change is very slow, and if pressed too strongly, it usually builds up still greater opposition. In particular, teachers tend to resist any change which leaves them with less control over their classrooms.

The attitudes and behaviour of teachers and administrators are functions both of their personalities and the institutions in which they work. Most organizations are designed for stability rather than change, and they seldom have mechanisms for changing themselves from within. Schools also reflect the concepts and values of their surrounding communities, and so can only try out new practices which have been fully accepted by most parents and legislators. Democratic relations between teacher and pupil, for example, are not already practised between parents and their children or between employers and employees.

Innovations are generated more often and accepted more readily by individuals with a number of common traits, which include self-confidence, willingness to take risks, youth, high social status, stronger than average contacts outside their immediate community and a tendency toward opinion leadership among their colleagues. Innovative teachers, in particular, are more self-confident, share more widely their experiences and information about teaching and are professionally more dedicated. Innovative institutions also have certain traits in common. They generally enjoy greater financial support, more highly trained teachers and more highly educated parents. They tend to be clearer about institutional goals, to have a good communications network amongst teachers and between teachers and administrators, to have a higher morale and greater cohesiveness, to invent new procedures or practices more often and to be more sensitive to new developments in research and policy. In particular, innovative schools devote resources over and above those required for normal operations to gaining knowledge of new concepts or methods and trying them out.

It is not possible to produce blueprints for bringing about innovations in education; hence we must concentrate on the factors which appear to favour or impede durable changes. A checklist of positive factors would include: proven quality, low cost, divisibility into parts, ease of communicability, low complexity, strong leadership or sponsorship, a favourable rather than neutral or inhibiting school or institutional environment, compatibility with the value and existing practices of adopters, effective mixture of rewards and punishments, readiness for change in the target system or group and the appropriateness of the proposed change to the surrounding community.

Studies of how educational changes take place in various settings have produced three paradigms. The 'research and development' model proceeds from theory to practice: innovations are conceived, initiated, incorporated and evaluated as part of an elaborate design supervised by a central planning agency. The 'social interaction' model follows the diffusion of the innovation among the members of a group or institution, and the 'problem solving' model interprets change from the point of view of the individual adopter. All three processes are at work to some degree in any innovation, but in particular national or local systems emphasize one another in their efforts to accelerate the passage from decision to application.

Similarly, authorities use different techniques for implementing change. The strategy generally used reflects the relationship between senior administrators and local teachers. In highly decentralized systems greater initiative is left to individuals to accept, refuse or modify the proposed changes. The major factor is less the authority of the person advocating the reform than the rationality and acceptability of the innovation itself. As a result, changes take longer but tend to be more durable. In highly centralized systems, innovations are enforced more often through a hierarchical chain of command, with psychological and economic sanctions against those who resist. Such reforms are applied more rapidly throughout the entire system, but they are seldom internalized by the adopters unless they are practised long enough to change habits and patterns of behaviour. The paradox, then, in managing change is that by involving the adopter, we are obliged to slow down or modify the original project — a situation which most technical experts, planners or senior administrators find unacceptable. When, however, a given change is at odds with the existing values and past experiences of the adopters, or is not in keeping with the structural properties of the receiving institution, it has little chance of success. Herein lies the crucial difference between changing things and changing persons, not to mention the inadvisability of using the same procedures for both.

Bibliography

1. Alexander, W.M. The acceleration of curriculum change. In: Miller, R., ed. *Perspectives on educational change*. New York, Appleton-Century-Crofts, 1967, p. 341-358.

2. Atwood, M.S. Small-scale administrative change: resistance to the introduction of a high school guidance program. In: Miles, M., ed. *Innovation in education*. New York, Teachers College Press, 1964, p. 49-78.

3. Barnett, H. *Innovation: the basis of cultural change*. New York, McGraw-Hill, 1953. 462 p., figs.

4. Beeby, C.E. *The quality of education in developing countries*. Cambridge, Mass., Harvard University Press, 1966. 139 p., bibl.

5. Bhola, H. *Innovation research and theory*. Columbus, Ohio, Ohio State University, 1965. 155 p.

6. Brickell, H. State organization for educational change: a case study and a proposal. In: Miles, M., ed. *Innovation in education*. New York, Teachers College Press, 1964, p. 493-532.

7. Brickell, H. Appraising the effects of innovation in local schooling. In: National Society for the Study of Education. *Educational evaluation, new roles, new means*. Chicago, Rand McNally, 1968, p. 284-304.

8. Buchanan, P. Crucial Issues in organizational development. In: Watson, G., ed. *Change in school systems*. Washington, National Training Laboratories, NEA, p. 51-67.

9. Carlson, R. *Adoption of educational innovations*. Eugene, Oregon, University of Oregon, [1965]. 84 p., figs.

10. Carlson, R. Barriers to change in public schools. In: *Change processes in the public schools*. Eugene, Oregon, University of Oregon, 1965, p. 3-10.

11. Centre for Educational Research and Innovation. Innovation in education. Part II: Report of the conference. Paris, Organisation for Economic Co-operation and Development, 1969. 66 p. [processed] (Document CERI/EI/69.22)

12. Chin, R; Benne K.D. General strategies for effecting changes in human systems. In: Bennis, W.G.; Benne, K.D.; Chin, R. *The planning of change*. New York, Holt, Rinehart and Winston, 1961, p. 32-59.

13. Coombs, P. *The world educational crisis*. New York, Praeger, 1968. 241 p.

14. Eichholz, G.; Rogers, E. Resistance to the adoption of audio-visual aids by elementary school teachers. In: Miles, M., ed. *Innovation in education*. New York, Teachers College Press, 1964, p. 299-316.

15. Fink, S.; Beak, J; Taddeo, K. Organizational crisis and change. In: *Journal of applied behavioural science* (Washington, D.C.), vol. 7, no. 1, 1971, p. 15-37.

16. Gallaher, A. The role of the advocate and directed change. In: Meierhenry, W., ed. *Media and educational innovation*. Lincoln, Nebr., University of Nebraska Press, [1964]. 445 p.

17. Gallaher, A. Directed change in formal organizations: the school system. In: Carlson, R.O., et al. *Change processes in the public schools*. Eugene, Oregon, University of Oregon, 1965. 92 p.

18. Griffiths, D. Administrative theory and change in organizations. In: Miles, M., ed. *Innovation in education*. New York, Teachers College Press, 1964, p. 425-436.

19. Guba, E. The process of educational innovation. In: Goulet, R., ed. *Educational change*. New York, Citation Press, 1968, p. 136-153.

20. Guba, E.; Clark, O. An examination of potential change roles in education. In: *Rational planning in curriculum and instruction*. Washington, D.C., National Education Association, 1967. 203 p.

21. Harvey, O. Conceptual systems and attitude change. In: Sherif, C.; Sherif, M. *Attitude, ego-involvement and change*. New York, J. Wiley, 1967, p. 201-226.

96

22. Havelock, R. *Guide to innovation in education*. Ann Arbor, Mich., University of Michigan, 1970. v.p.

23. Havelock, R. *Planning for innovation through dissemination and utilization of knowledge*. Ann Arbor, Mich., University of Michigan, 1971. v.p.

24. Hilfiker, L. *Relationship of school system innovativeness to selected dimensions of interpersonal behavior in eight school systems*. Madison, Wisc., Center for Cognitive Learning, 1969. 67 p., figs., bibl.

25. Jung, C. The trainer change-agent role within a school system In: Watson, G., ed. *Change in school systems*. Washington, D.C., National Training Laboratories, NEA, 1967, p. 89-105.

26. Jung, C.; Fox R.; Lippitt, R. An orientation and strategy for working on problems of change in school systems. In: Watson, G., ed. *Change in school systems*. Washington, D.C., National Training Laboratories, NEA, 1967, p. 68-88.

27. Katz, E. Diffusion of new ideas and practices. In: Schramm, W., ed. *The science of human communication: new directions and new findings in communication research*. New York, Basic Books [1963]. 158 p.

28. Lippitt, R. The teacher as innovator, seeker and sharer of new practices. In: Miller, R., ed. *Perspectives on educational change*. New York, Appleton-Century-Crofts, 1967, p. 307-324.

29. Lippitt, R. Improving the socialization process. In: Watson, G., ed. *Change in school systems*. Washington, D.C., National Training Laboratories, NEA 1967, p. 30-50.

30. Lionberger, H. The diffusion research tradition in rural sociology and its relation to implemented change in public school systems. In: Meierhenry, W., ed. *Media and educational innovation*. Lincoln, Nebr., University of Nebraska, [1964], p. 111-156.

31. Maguire, L. *Observations and analysis of the literature on change*. Philadelphia, Research for Better Schools, 1970. 46 p.

32. MacKenzie, G. Curricular change: participants, power and processes. In: Miles, M., ed. *Innovation in education*. New York, Teachers College Press, 1964, p. 399-424.

33. Marsh, P. Wellsprings of strategy: considerations affecting innovations by the PSSC. In: Miles, M., ed. *Innovation in education*. New York, Teachers College Press, 1964, p. 249-270.

34. Meadows, P. Novelty and acceptors: a sociological consideration of the acceptance of change. In: Meierhenry, W., ed. *Media and educational innovation*. Lincoln, Nebr., University of Nebraska, [1964], p. 51-85.

35. Miles, M. Educational innovation: the nature of the problem. In: Miles, M., ed. *Innovation in education*. New York, Teachers College Press, 1964, p. 1-48.

36. Miles, M. On temporary systems. In: Miles, M., ed. *Innovation in education*. New York, Teachers College Press, 1964, p. 437-492.

37. Miles, M. Innovation in education: some generalizations. In: Miles, M., ed. *Innovation in education*. New York, Teachers College Press, 1964, p. 631-662.

38. Miles, M. Planned change and organizational health: figure and ground. In: *Change processes in the public schools*. Eugene, Ore.; University of Oregon, 1964, p. 11-36.

39. Miles, M. Some properties of schools as social systems. In: Watson, G., ed. *Change in school systems*, Washington D.C., National Training Laboratories, NEA, 1967, p. 1-29.

40. Miller, R. Some observations and suggestions. In: Miller, R., ed. *Perspectives on educational change*. New York, Appleton-Century-Crofts, 1967, p. 359-386.

41. Mort, P. Studies in educational innovation from the Institute of Administrative Research. In: Miles, M., ed. *Innovation in education*. New York, Teachers College Press, 1964, p. 317-328.

42. Pellegrin, R. The place of research in planned change. In: *Change processes in the public schools*. Eugene, Ore.; University of Oregon, 1965, p. 65-78.

43. Reichart, S. *Change and the teacher: the philosophy of a social phenomenon*. New York, T. Crowell, [1969]. 151 p.

44. Richland, M. Traveling seminar and conference for the implementation of educational innovations. Santa Monica, Calif, Systems Develpment Corp., 1965. 144 p. [processed]

45. Rogers, C. *On becoming a person: a therapist's view of psycho-therapy*. Boston, Houghton-Mifflin, 1961. 420 p. bibl., illus.

46. Rogers, E. *Diffusion of innovations*. New York, Free Press, 1962. 367 p.

47. Rogers, E. What are innovators like. In: Carlson, R.O., et al., *Change processes in the public schools*. Eugene, Ore., University of Oregon, 1965, p. 55-64.

48. Rubin, L. Installing an innovation. In: Goulet, R., ed. *Educational change*. New York, Citation Press, 1968, p. 154-168.

49. Schon, D. *Technology and change*. New York, Dell Publishing Co., 1967. 248 p.

50. Spindler, G. *Education and culture: anthropological approaches*. New York, Holt, Rinehart and Winston, 1963. 571 p.

51. Steiner, G. *The creative organization*. Chicago, University of Chicago Press, [1965]. 267 p.

52. Sussman, L. *Innovation in education: United States*. Paris, OECD, 1971. 67 p. [processed] (Document CERI/EI/71.05)

53. Toffler, A. *Future Shock*. New York: Random House, 1970.

54. Trow, M. Methodological problems in the evaluation of innovation. In: Wittrock, M.C.; Wiley, D.E., eds. *Evaluation of instruction*. New York, Holt, Rinehart and Winston, 1970, p. 289-305.

55. Watson, G. Toward a conceptual architecture of a self-renewing school system. In: Watson, G., ed. *Change in school systems*, Washington, D.C., National Training Laboratories, NEA, 1967, p. 106-115.

56. Westley, W. Report of a conference. In: *Inovation in education*, part one. Paris, OECD, 1969. 55 p. [processed] (Document CERI/EI/69.19)

Questionnaire

To develop the series further, it would be helpful if readers could record their impressions and inform the IBE. (Please write 'yes' or 'no' in the space following each question. Further comments may be written on the back of this sheet.)

1. Do you find the author's analysis useful for your own work?   in particular, is it:
   - an adequate survey of the field?
   - a basis for further discussion and study?
   - too abstract to be useful?

2. With regard to the sources cited, could you indicate any recent documents of a similar type which have been overlooked?

3. Can you indicate any cases of innovation in your own country (or field of specialization) which you feel might have inter- est for other countries if adequately written up? Please name the person or institution able to provide further information about the project.

Please indicate your name and address and return this questionnaire to: the International Bureau of Education, Palais Wilson, 1211 Geneva 14, Switzerland or, when applicable, to your Unesco Regional Office for Education (i.e. Bankok, Dakar or Santiago).

Questionnaire